CONVERSATIONS WITH PEOPLE WHO HATE ME

CONVERSATIONS WITH PEOPLE WHO HATE ME

12 Things I Learned from Talking to Internet Strangers

DYLAN MARRON

ATRIA BOOKS

NEW YORK   LONDON   TORONTO   SYDNEY   NEW DELHI

ATRIA
BOOKS

An Imprint of Simon & Schuster, Inc.
1230 Avenue of the Americas
New York, NY 10020

First Atria Books hardcover edition March 2022

ATRIA B O O K S and colophon are trademarks of
Simon & Schuster, Inc.

For information about special discounts for bulk purchases,
please contact Simon & Schuster Special Sales at 1-866-506-1949
or business@simonandschuster.com.

The Simon & Schuster Speakers Bureau can bring authors to
your live event. For more information or to book an event,
contact the Simon & Schuster Speakers Bureau at 1-866-248-3049
or visit our website at www.simonspeakers.com.

Interior design by Kathryn A. Kenney-Peterson

Manufactured in the United States of America

1 3 5 7 9 10 8 6 4 2

Library of Congress Cataloging-in-Publication Data is available.

ISBN 978-1-9821-2927-9
ISBN 978-1-9821-2929-3 (ebook)

For my mom, who always taught me
to walk toward conflict and not away from it.

CONTENTS

AUTHOR'S NOTE

A few years ago, I began a social experiment in which I phoned my internet detractors and engaged them in conversation. This concept grew, and soon enough I was moderating discussions between others who had clashed online as well. I've published many of these calls through my podcast *Conversations with People Who Hate Me*.

This book tells the story of this social experiment, the events that precipitated it, the mistakes I've made along the way, and the twelve lessons I learned throughout the process. Each chapter is one of these lessons. I have learned far more than twelve things, and I trust there are many things that I'm not even yet aware that I learned—seeds that are still sprouting in the garden of my mind— but we all have stuff to do and places to be, so I cut it down to a dozen of my most salient takeaways so we can all get on with our beautiful lives.

The dialogue in this book has been verified by recordings and message archives. For the few brief conversations that have no record, I have re-created them from memory and consulted my conversation partner to confirm that my retelling matches their memory, too.

There are seven guests from my podcast whose conversations I spotlight in this book. All of them—with the exception of a public figure—are referred to pseudonymously. Some aliases correspond with the name these guests used on the podcast, others do not.

Comments and messages that I quote have been fact-checked against screenshots. Typos have, for the most part, been left in. However, a few details have been intentionally altered for the purpose of further anonymizing some of the people I mention.

You are welcome to read this book as a guide on how to navigate difficult conversations of your own, or as a distant story that happened to someone once. Take what serves you and leave what doesn't.

You may see yourself reflected in me, or perhaps you will see your reflection in the people who called me a "moron," a "piece of shit," and told me to "killlllllllllllllllllllllllll [my]self." Maybe it's a mix of both. Or maybe you won't identify with anyone mentioned in this book at all and wonder if there's something wrong with you. (There isn't.)

Whatever the case may be, welcome. I'm thrilled to have you here. Let's get started.

CONVERSATIONS
WITH PEOPLE
WHO HATE ME

1

the internet is a game

"People hate me," I say, slumping in my chair.

"Yeah, I've been meaning to tell you: I hate you," Ethan jokes.

I half smile, more to acknowledge that a joke was made than anything else. Really, I'm just grateful to be talking to a real human being rather than the digital ones I interact with every day. After months of receiving a steady stream of negative comments and messages, homophobic jabs, and a handful of death threats, it has all become too much to bear.

"I'm really sorry," he says, scrunching his nose to offset this moment of sincerity.

We're sitting in Ethan's office on the thirty-fifth floor of a building in midtown Manhattan, where he oversees Seriously.TV, the digital television network where I've been writing and producing short, topical comedy videos for the last six months. Our offices don't look like the typically sleek headquarters of a startup media enterprise. If it weren't for the production equipment in the halls and the scripts lining his desk, a passerby might not even realize this was a media outlet at all. The furniture that surrounds us seems to have been inherited from a corporate bank, as the generic patterns and high-gloss cherrywood are better suited to talk of investments and portfolios than joke punch-ups and sketch pitches.

My phone pings and I look down to see a notification. Immediately, I tap it, as I have been well trained to do.

"Your page has a new message," it reads. Like a good user, I click to open it.

"Youre a moron. Youre the reason this country is dividing itself. All your videos are meerly opinion, and an awful opinion i must say. Just stop. Plus being Gay is a sin."

The cruel irony of getting a hate message while talking to my boss about the influx of hate messages is not lost on me. Wordlessly I show it to Ethan, illuminating his face with the dull white glow of my phone. He sits back after reading it, takes a beat, and then, in cartoonish shock, exclaims: "Wait . . . you're gay?!"

"Don't tell my husband."

He laughs. This is our little bit. But I'm only performing it out of memory and Ethan can tell. He exhales and rubs his forehead. "I think this is just what comes with the territory."

I nod and look off into the distance.

"Look, I'm really sorry," he says. "I don't know what to say."

"Yeah," I reply because no one ever knows what to say. Not my friends, not my husband Todd, not my boss, not even me.

"Well, *I* think you're great."

"Thanks, Ethan." Then, cocking my head to the side, I roll my eyes, and, in a Muppet-like underwater garble, I say, "I think you're great, too."

"Now get out of here! And don't ever come back!" He points a dramatic finger to the door, with an emphasized underbite like a cartoon villain.

I laugh, get up, leave his office, and stand outside his door for a moment so I can reopen the message I've just received. I begin my ritual: *Take a screenshot. View profile. Scroll. View photos. Next. Next.*

Next. Back to profile. Scroll. Scroll. Scroll. I do this each time I receive a message like this, which has recently been quite often. In the seconds it takes to complete this ritual, I learn the name, hometown, and workplace of the sender. This sender's name is Josh. Josh is in high school, a senior from what I can tell. He works at Best Buy. Josh has recently gotten a haircut. "What do yall think?" he asks in the photo's caption. According to the memes that he's shared, it seems that we unsurprisingly support different candidates in the 2016 presidential election that's just over one month away.

I know what's about to happen. I know I will put Josh's message in a digital folder that sits on my computer's desktop. I know that in that folder his message will join countless others just like it, all written by other internet strangers who seem to hate me. What I *don't* know, though, is that this one message, and this one stranger, will soon spark a change within me, prompting me to reconsider everything I thought I knew about the internet, disagreement, and conversation itself.

I. TRAINING

This is my dream job. I get to make creative work on the internet about issues that matter to me, all while grinding alongside others who are doing the same. The consequences of this job—namely, the onslaught of hate—may be overwhelming, but I'm not going to give up now. I can't. I spent the last half-decade consciously working toward an opportunity like this and I'm not going to let it go.

Four years earlier, I was cast as an ensemble member of a downtown performance art collective called the New York Neo-Futurists—Neos, for short—whose signature weekly show had us performing thirty short pieces in one hour. Because of their length—around two minutes each—some audience members would mistakenly call these pieces "sketches," which we were quick to correct: These were not sketches, they were *plays*. Sketches, we explained, were filled with tightly written jokes and featured characters. We never wrote jokes; our comedy came from the tasks we forced ourselves to do. And we never played characters, we only performed as ourselves. This is because there was one rule we followed: We couldn't lie. Everything we wrote and every task we performed had to be true. If one short play was titled *I Am Going to Call an Ex and Tell Them Why I Miss Them*, then, live on stage, the performer would actually have to dial up a former partner and, in front of the audience, tell them why they missed them. A confessional monologue about facing arachnophobia had to be honest. If the performer decided to confront a spider each night, then that spider would have to be real. But honesty didn't mean everything had to be serious, so another play might feature the entire ensemble performing a tightly choreographed dance to the recorded sounds of a subway platform remixed over a syncopated beat. (Those recorded sounds, though, would have to be real.)

Each week I had to write new plays and this ongoing assignment taught me to take stock of everything around me, interrogate exactly how I felt about it, and translate that feeling into art. I soon began to process daily life as a series of prompts, and I met each of these prompts with a question: *What am I going to do about it?* Through this lens every experience, every observation, every cry, and every triumph became inspiration. A mean customer at my restaurant job, *What am I going to do about it?* The sounds of Brooklyn as I walked home after working a dinner shift, *What am I going to do about it?* An unrequited crush, *What am I going to do about it?*

I loved this work and poured myself into it for years, waiting tables during the day and then running to the theater at night. After shows I would take the late train home and soar through the tunnels beneath the city, savoring the connection I had just made with a few dozen people. I grew as an artist, as a writer, and as a person, too. Creating work for a live audience was intimate, and it was this intimacy that gave theater its magic, a magic that I was invited to witness and revel in night after night. But this intimacy was also a limitation. A wildly successful, sold-out performance of our weekly show meant that it would only ever be seen by ninety-nine people. The long-form play I spent half a year writing was attended by just over a thousand audience members in its three-week run. I knew that good art did not need to be popular, but I also knew that audience size meant stability. And if I indeed wanted to turn my creative work into a full-time job, as I so badly did, then an audience is precisely what I would have to find. I just didn't know how. Fortunately, I was surrounded by other artists working toward the same goal.

The company was a community of ensemble members and their friends, partners, and outside collaborators, and the members of this community were always up to something. Some facilitated morning dance raves, others produced short experimental films, while a couple were boldly exploring new forms of media. Joseph Fink and Jeffrey Cranor had been quietly tinkering on a podcast that was narrated by fellow ensemble member Cecil Baldwin. The show, a fictional radio broadcast from a nonexistent desert town, was called *Welcome to Night Vale*, and when it unexpectedly soared to number one on the iTunes podcast charts in the summer of 2013, we all celebrated their success. I was pleasantly shocked that a show whose scripts were written on Google Docs, recorded with forty-dollar microphones into free software, and, best of all, was created by hard-working people I loved, had become the most popular podcast in the United States. This made everything seem possible and I cheered on their success from the sidelines, until one day when I was invited onto the field. "Do you want to be part of our little show?" Jeffrey asked me in an email. "Do you want to play Carlos?" I immediately knew what an honor this was. Carlos was the narrator's love interest and was so beloved by the podcast's growing listener base he would often appear in various fan art posted to Tumblr. What's more, he and Cecil were a rare source of queer, interracial representation in sci-fi storytelling. "of COURSE??!" I scream-typed back in response. A few months later, I joined them on their first West Coast tour where in the hour before each performance, I would stand in the wings as the theater doors opened so I could hear the distant murmurs of incoming audience members grow into a roar. Through the curtains I was able to catch glimpses of digital friends meeting in person for the first time. A community was being formed through a podcast.

As *Welcome to Night Vale*'s reach expanded, the tours grew longer, too. And it was in the postshow meet-and-greets that I was able to speak with young fans who quietly confided in me truths they had yet to tell their parents. "I just wanted to let you know," a fan once whispered to me while their dad patiently waited a few feet away, "Cecil and Carlos are very important to me, if you know what I mean." They trailed off, surreptitiously gesturing at their awaiting parent. "So, I guess, thanks." At each stop, similar hushed confessions were delivered to us, and each time we would get the growing sense that we were doing much more than simply welcoming audience members to a fictional southwestern town. To some, we were offering a possibility of what might be. I would often float to my hotel room after these interactions, marveling that this show, that this moment, all got to exist because of the internet.

Each performance to a sold-out crowd of thousands yielded an incredible rush, but this success was not my success. It was someone else's and I worried that I was an undeserving beneficiary. I longed to make my own piece of popular work, and the way I thought to do that was by getting an agent. Upon returning from a cross-country tour, I used whatever connections I could to set up meetings with potential representatives.

I'd had these meetings before. Ten years earlier, while I was still in high school, potential agents would call me into their offices, praise me for my talent, and then tell me how unlikely I was to get work. "You're so," they would all say, searching for the word "*specific.*" This was a euphemism that the industry used to mean "too diverse," and it was often applied to anyone who dared to occupy multiple marginalized identities at the same time.

Now, however, in 2015, I was sure that I would get an agent in no time. How could I not? I was finishing a successful tour with a popular podcast, and I had just been nominated for a prestigious theater award for a play I had written months earlier. Surely, they would be chomping at the bit to work with me. Strangely though, none of them were. As a teenager, I had accepted all of their feedback as objective truth, but now that I was essentially being told the same thing as an adult, I refused to accept it. Agents were signing friends with far less experience. Desperate for clarity, I started looking at casting notices, and only then could I begin to understand why they were hesitant to sign me.

One casting notice for a film might read: "RYAN, YOUNG 30s. SHY. STUDIED LITERATURE IN COLLEGE BUT NOW WORKS AT A DIGITAL STARTUP. LOST BUT TRYING TO FIND HIMSELF. AN EMPATH."

Another for the same film could read: "DELI WORKER. MIDDLE EASTERN, BLACK, LATINO, OR ASIAN. SELLS RYAN A SANDWICH BEFORE HIS BIG MEETING. 5 LINES."

What I thought was a personal failure, I was now beginning to understand to be a much larger systemic issue. There were simply far fewer roles for non-white people. Signing me as a client would just be a bad business decision on their part. So, agentless and frustrated, I turned to my reliable prompt: *What am I going to do about it?*

A year earlier I had written a short piece for the Neos' weekly show in which I performed every line spoken by a person of color in a popular romantic comedy. There were just a handful of lines, all spoken by an underused Latina actress who played a supporting character's maid. The piece's brevity would send the audience into fits of laughter, and as that laughter subsided, I could hear them consider the darker insinuation. Guffaws turned to groans which gave way to gasps. It was, I found, a perfect way to share an idea: Wrap it in laughter so the medicine goes down easier. I began to think of this as "candied kale." Nutrition wrapped in sugar. A lesson, coated in entertainment. Now I just needed to make that idea bigger. Perhaps, I thought, I could apply this idea to other films, but rather than performing the lines myself I would edit down the actual footage to only the words spoken by actors of color. It would be time-consuming but with an entire summer stretched out before me and not a single agent interested in signing me, I figured I had nothing to lose.

Day after day, I sat in my bedroom, hunched over my laptop, whittling down feature-length films to a handful of seconds. The entire 558-minute *The Lord of the Rings* trilogy was cut down to 46 seconds, 0.14 percent of its cumulative runtime. *Maleficent*, the live-action Disney spin-off of *Sleeping Beauty* featured only an unnamed captain and ran at 18 seconds. The popular movie-musical *Into the Woods* featured no speaking roles for actors of color at all. My methodology was simple: Select movies that told universal stories that simply were cast as white by default. *The Lord of the Rings* was about the epic quest for a ring. *Maleficent* was about a misunderstood godmother. *Into the Woods* told the story of a witch who forced a baker and his wife to traipse through an enchanted forest and collect items from recognizable fairy-tale characters. None of these movies were about race, per se, nor were these stories inherently white, yet they were told with all white actors.

I called the series *Every Single Word*, fashioned a logo on Microsoft Word, and began sharing the videos on my YouTube channel. After only a few weeks, the project gained traction. First, there was a story in *Slate*. Then *BuzzFeed*. Then the *Washington Post*. Then *All Things Considered*. Soon enough, the series was seemingly everywhere. I couldn't believe that a project I had made in my bedroom was reaching millions of viewers and that its intended takeaway was actually coming through. "I never realized this," people would say to me about the disproportionate racial representation on screen. "Now I can't unsee it."

I had finally made a project that spoke to a large audience. A creation that spotlighted an issue far bigger than me. It was this democratization of the internet that thrilled me. Social media did away with gatekeepers, so now regular people like me didn't have to wait for permission to speak their minds. We, the people, could stand up to a public figure and finally be heard. I wanted to do this forever. To keep using the internet to talk about social issues in accessible formats. To keep making candied kale.

Ironically, a series that was inspired by agents' lack of interest had sparked a flurry of requests. So when my new agent, Kaitlyn, sent me an audition for a digital television network that would release short, shareable videos throughout the day to quickly comment on news stories, I leapt at the opportunity. There couldn't have been a more perfect job for me. This position would call upon the writing practice I developed for the Neos, the internet fluency I gained from *Night*

Vale, and the socially conscious mission I established with *Every Single Word*. When Kaitlyn told me I got the job, I cried. And when I showed up to my first day at Seriously.TV, two weeks later, I was ready to devote myself fully.

On my first day I was given a tour of their—*our*—facilities. The studio, a converted storage closet, was tiny for my new coworkers coming from the television world but enormous for my experimental performance art background. I excitedly shook hands with the team of talented editors and camera operators who would run the technical side of production, and counted my blessings that every day I would be able to wake up, scan the news, ask myself *What am I going to do about it?* and an entire team of experts would answer that question with me.

II. RULES

I was determined to master this new terrain. Seriously.TV's videos would be released primarily on Facebook, and whereas *Welcome to Night Vale* was a cult hit for those who knew about it, and *Every Single Word* was celebrated in the socially progressive enclaves of Tumblr, now I would be speaking to the internet at large and not just one of its breakout rooms. This was April of 2016. The presidential primaries were in full swing, a culture war was just beginning to brew in the news cycle, and social media was becoming the new public square. This platform was a privilege and I resolved to use it for good. I even had a clear goal: Spark vital conversations about social issues, educate the masses, and mitigate conflict through knowledge. And so, in the free moments between script deadlines, lunch breaks, and train transfers, I closely studied the internet, eager to optimize my videos to reach as many people as possible.

I needed to figure out how to be relevant. But the conversation erupting every day on social media was a constantly evolving, amorphous blob, a shape-shifting mechanical bull that took precision and talent to ride. The internet seemed to have an opinion about everything, and all of those opinions were broadcast at the same time and at the same volume. Personal grievances were published alongside impassioned pleas for justice. Vulnerable confessions were woven between mundane observations, and the rest of the cyber real estate was dedicated to joke memes, carefully curated apathy, and the messy airing of dirty laundry. To be relevant, I would have to focus on whatever was most talked about that day online.

I needed to figure out who I was speaking to. But an infinite stream of people zoomed past me on the digital highways and byways of social media, and it became too overwhelming to think of each of these passing pixels as individual human beings, so I started thinking of those little grainy profile pictures as "everyone." My audience was no longer a collection of specific individuals that I could see in the dim light of the theater. Now it was all the people watching all the time. This was an endless auditorium. And it was exactly where I wanted to be.

But this endless auditorium was pretty noisy, so I needed to figure out how to be heard. "DO BETTER!" internet activists were shouting in posts, comment sections, and sometimes literally in tweets that said just that. These two words seemed to slice through the noise faster than a meticulously edited op-ed, or a carefully researched book. If I screamed loudly enough with my caps lock key, it seemed like The Powers That Be would listen. "THIS DEMANDS YOUR ATTENTION" seemed to be an effective way to identify anything from a local nuisance to a systemic miscarriage of justice. Bold declarations and simple mandates traveled way further and faster than soft questions or nuanced considerations. Wrestling with the complexities of a certain topic was fine and good, but the way to skyrocket through the algorithm was to say something in black and white: *This* was good, and *that* was bad. *This* was right, and *that* was wrong.

To truly succeed on the internet I would need to adapt to its demands. I loved the fervor with which people were speaking and the intensity with which they defended their ideas. Everyone finally had a voice and together our voices formed a chorus. Each tweet, post, and video became an opportunity, a personal press release that reported on every feeling and thought I might have. And since I was here to make candied kale, I resolved to use my platform as a voice for the marginalized against The Powers That Be. I was on the side of progressivism and social justice, so it followed that The Powers That Be in question were conservatism and anything else that may have gone against the edicts of social justice.

I came to see myself as a David, fighting an army of Goliaths on behalf of other, smaller Davids. Luckily, the internet produced a new Goliath every day, a new opponent to defeat, and whether it was a corrupt system or a private citizen who erred, my fellow Davids and I were always up for the task. After a lifetime of not quite belonging, I finally was unquestionably part of a movement larger than myself. An army. A team. A side. Change, real change, was finally within reach.

Now that I had a clear enemy, the relentless news cycle was no longer a cacophony of catastrophes, but an endless supply of prompts, one that always provided an injustice that I could seek to correct. When Donald Trump made a comment that Hillary Clinton was playing the "woman's card," I made a satirical ad for this nonexistent product with my coworker Mary. When the actor Kirk Cameron said that "wives are to honor and respect and follow their husband's lead" to the *Christian Post*, I filmed a sketch where I played a Kirk Cameron defender whose wife was revealed to be a literal puppet. And when North Carolina's Governor Pat McCrory signed a bill that sought to ban transgender people from using the bathroom that aligned with their gender identity, I asked myself: *What am I going to do about it?*

Like many fear-based laws, North Carolina's bathroom bill was disguised in the seemingly well-intentioned mission to protect women and children. Hateful legislation depended on fear, and fear grew from the unknown. I wanted to reverse that. What I came up with was a weekly series where I would interview my trans friends in the bathroom that aligned with their gender identity. I titled this series *Sitting in Bathrooms with Trans People* and in a makeshift studio in one of our floor's two restrooms, I would ask my guests about the expected topics—like, when they decided to transition and how they began understanding their identity—but also the mundane: favorite snacks, boring pastimes, and the guilty pleasure reality shows they watched in secret. With each interview, I was attempting to chip away at the harm caused by these laws. So when the series' first episode became Seriously.TV's first video to get one hundred thousand views, and the first to attract media attention, I couldn't help but see each view, each piece of coverage, as a dent in transphobia itself. My numerical success was now directly tied to the amount of good I thought I was bringing to the world.

And if my view counts were directly tied to progress, then I wanted to push my metrics even higher. To do that I would finally have to address my Achilles' heel: earnestness. All of my work up to this point—the Tumblr posts I would write to *Night Vale* fans about coming out of the closet, or navigating my biracial identity, the *Every Single Word* speeches I gave about racial representation on screen, even the soft comedy of *Sitting in Bathrooms with Trans People*— reflected my authentic voice, which was deeply earnest and sincere.

Unfortunately, I was learning that this was a cardinal sin on the wider internet. In fact, many public confessions of something as simple as liking a book or enjoying the company of a loved one were preceded by "Earnest post alert!" as a sort of trigger warning that an unfiltered feeling was about to be shared. I couldn't quite understand why. Was it because apathy, snark, and sarcasm were more in keeping with the onslaught of bad news that dominated our news cycle? Did public expressions of joy undercut the severity of the unfolding sociopolitical mess? Whatever the reason, I had to figure out how to maintain my success on a platform that would shun me for daring to express my true self. The only positivity that seemed to be allowed was what I came to call "gruesome positivity." Saying you had an amazing weekend with your family was far too Hallmark-y, while saying you had an amazing weekend with your sworn enemy was acceptably subversive. "Ooh! I really love this actor," however true it may be, sounded too simple. On the other hand, "step on my neck daddy" invoked a sadomasochistic desire to be ruined as a way to disguise any feelings of real joy. Paradoxically, sincerity came off as insincere on the internet, and snark sounded more honest. I knew if I wanted to really succeed I would have to sharpen my jabs, and trade in my proverbial wool sweater for barbed wire armor. So, on a late May afternoon when I came across a viral video of a young conservative woman taking our generation to task, I was sure I had found my opportunity to try out a new, more biting tone.

The woman in the widely shared video was Alexis Bloomer, and her bright green eyes looked directly into the camera as she sat in the driver's seat of her parked car listing the reasons that millennials—her generation and mine—weren't living up to the standards of our elders. "Our generation doesn't have the basic manners that include 'no, ma'am,' and 'yes, ma'am,'" she said. "We don't even hold the door open for ladies, much less our elders anymore." My ears perked up, knowing that a harkening back to "the good old days" was a dog whistle that harmonized with Donald Trump's "Make America Great Again" slogan. A Goliath had presented itself and I had a new voice to sharpen, so I picked up my digital slingshot and quickly wrote a script that responded to her points one by one.

"We use words like 'bae' to describe someone we love," she said in her video.

"And *we* use words like 'racist' to describe someone who thinks that the word 'bae' isn't real simply because it didn't originate from a white eurocentric vernacular," I typed back in my script.

"Now I guess I see why people call us 'Generation Y,'" she said into her camera.

"Because it comes after '*x*' and before '*z*' and that's how the alphabet works," I planned to bite back into mine.

The next morning, I recorded my lines staring directly into my phone's camera, imagining that I was addressing Alexis directly. I employed a more sarcastic and patronizing tone than I was used to, the same voice a parent might employ with their child when asking "Are you sure you did the dishes, mister?" while looking at a pile of dirty plates in the sink. By directing my biting comebacks to an imagined hologram of my conservative counterpart, I was emboldened to cut harder than I ever would have if she had been directly across from me.

Within twenty-four hours of my video being posted it had amassed over a million views, becoming the first Seriously.TV video to reach such a milestone. I couldn't unglue my eyes from the skyrocketing digits in the bottom left hand corner of the screen. And as the numbers kept climbing, it was as though I was taking a hit not just at Alexis Bloomer, but at conservatism itself. In my mind, the two became the same. Alexis was conservatism and conservatism was Alexis.

Right beside the rapidly rising view count was the comment section. Supporters said kind things in response and championed me for taking her down. "OMG YESSS thank you for this cuz her video is straight trash!" one user wrote on my page. "Lol been waitin for a good clapback and you delivered!" But, for the first time, I had critics. Many critics, it seemed. "I really want to bitchslap some reality in his ass," one person wrote. Another man called me a "whiny little bitch." "He literally was cancer," said one user in his review of the video. But this criticism was so novel that rather than being offended, I was flattered that I mattered enough to hate.

The numerical success of this video was undeniable, so I meticulously reviewed all that I had done differently in order to duplicate its success in the future.

By donning a more sarcastic tone, I was able to cut through the noise of the internet and speak its language. By responding to an already-viral video, I was ensuring my own video's relevance. By providing clips of her video, passersby didn't need to know any backstory. By keeping the format a simple back-and-forth between setup and punch line, I lowered the barrier to entry. But perhaps the biggest factor in this video's success was that I had a clear opponent. This gave my viewers a show. Alexis and I were even visually coded as oppositional: She was a blond, conventionally attractive, "all-American" white woman who looked like she could be the poster girl for the Republican party, and I was a brown, Mohawked, pearl-earring-wearing gay guy whose tank top revealed an upper body that clearly screamed "chosen last for dodgeball."

In listing the factors that I presumed led to this video's virality, I had inadvertently created a set of rules that I could follow for all future videos: Be aggressive, seize on trending topics, provide all necessary context, keep it simple, and have an opponent. And to consider these edicts as rules allowed me to see the internet as a game. Once I understood that, everything else fit into place.

The likes, shares, and views that I chased were the points I could accrue. The news stories I encountered were the challenges I had to complete. Each video was a new level, and the success of one would unlock the next. And, like a video game, I was playing as an avatar, a snarkier, more biting version of myself. My avatar looked like me, had the same name as me, but he was not fully me. His words were scripted, his sentences edited and crisp. My avatar was ruthless, which was good because games can be won or lost—and I was determined to win.

After all, I was in pursuit of a noble goal: to defeat injustice everywhere. Time was of the essence so I traded the contemplative *What am I going to do about it?* for the more efficient *What's the funniest way I can destroy this right now?* Each day was a new "go" at this obstacle course, another opportunity to beat yesterday's score, and I was having a blast as I did it.

Throughout the summer of 2016 I was on a winning streak, taking prompts from the news cycle and spinning them into satire, reaping the rewards each time I released a video. I made short PSAs that mocked faulty conservative logic, I wrote direct-to-camera essays that exposed hypocrisy, and I covered the RNC and DNC as a correspondent. As August approached, I wanted to build myself a regular weekly sketch series.

I had become particularly enthralled by the popularity of unboxing videos, a YouTube genre where an on-camera personality opens up a new gadget and shows off its components to their audience. So I decided to satirize it. Instead of unboxing the latest smartphone or gaming console, I would crack open intangible ideologies as if they were products. That meant unboxing the "Mistreatment of Native Americans" and finding a globe with an accompanying Wite-Out, in order to "erase already existing and thriving regions so that you can visit them, reclaim them, and then rename them after yourself." When I unboxed "Masculinity" I pulled out a hazmat suit and gas mask to avoid the toxins that would inevitably emanate from the package. And when I opened up "Police Brutality" I performed my cartoonish shock when I couldn't find an indictment in the box, as if it was a component that should have been included but wasn't.

I released two or three videos per week and this frequency allowed me to get better and better at the game, ensuring a weekly deposit of likes, shares, comments, and views into my ever-growing pot of points. But as with every game there was, I learned, a way to lose points, too.

As my videos grew in popularity, so too did the hate in response. With each unlocked level, crushed opponent, and new follower, there came a detractor ready to pounce, lurking around every corner, and hiding in every comment section. What was first a novelty quickly became a troubling infestation and, instinctively, I started taking screenshots of as many pieces of hate as I could and collected these comments, messages, and tweets in a desktop bin I aptly labeled HATE FOLDER.

Some of the HATE FOLDER screenshots were amusing, like the ones that took swipes at my masculinity. The comments that called me a "faggot" were always delightful. They were kind of like calling a whale a whale. Sure, this might hurt another mammal who doesn't want to be called a whale, but a whale would be like "Yes, that's me. May I help you?" The word "cuck" was also frequently thrown at me. It was an abbreviated version of *cuckold*, a slur for men who had been cheated on by their wives and I always wondered how this was meant to offend me, as I surely would encourage my hypothetical wife to cheat on me and get the physical touch I couldn't offer. I was often labeled a "beta male," too, the derogatory term for weak men who weren't strong enough to be alphas, but even beta was generous. Maybe gamma male or even delta male would have been a more accurate approximation of what I was, as I proudly lived so beneath the bar that society had set for masculine paradigms. Anytime I threw a basketball, hammered a nail, or carried anything over five pounds was proof that my mere existence was a performance art piece in opposition to masculinity.

Of course, this amusement was only a shield to act like these comments didn't hurt. When I received these pieces of hate I did not meet them with quick comebacks or smart retorts. When someone named Valentin told me I was "a disgrace to humanity," I felt horrible. When an anonymous Twitter account tweeted out "On a scale of 1 to GRIDS"—gay-related immunodeficiency, the outdated term for AIDS, with an extra 's' thrown on for flare—"how gay is @dylanmarron?" . . . I didn't have any joke in response, just sadness and the horror that someone could write that. I didn't even know what to do with the two-word message I received that just said, "dumb fag."

Online hate was a relatively new phenomenon, a problem that no one really knew how to deal with quite yet, so I didn't have many tools to process it. At first, I chose not to talk about it at all, figuring this was a champagne problem that was best left ignored. Then, when I no longer could keep it to myself, I went the opposite direction: talking about it nonstop to anyone who would listen.

My husband, Todd, was just beginning his first year of law school three states away, which meant that I could only ever process the daily HATE FOLDER additions with him on quick phone calls in between his classes or on the weekends when we would see each other. He always gave me the time and space to vent, carefully listening to every convoluted theory and observation I frantically shared no matter how many times I had said it before, and he would always supportively say, "I'm so sorry, sweetie. What can I do to help?" But I didn't know the answer.

At drinks with friends I would read aloud the funniest additions to the HATE FOLDER, as a hybrid form of therapy and entertainment. Invariably my friends would put down the authors of the posts. "Fuck those trolls," they would say defensively. "They're just sad, lonely people." And each of my friends prescribed the same remedy: "Just log off!" But this prescription was much easier to dole out than it was to take. The internet was essentially my workplace. Logging off wouldn't be that easy. Plus, I was in the middle of playing the game and succeeding. How could I stop now?

Paradoxically, I despised the HATE FOLDER's existence but also couldn't look away. Not talking about it didn't help. Talking about it didn't really help, either. Trapped in this predicament, I found there was only one thing that truly soothed me: imagining the kindest possible version of the people behind the hate.

Because most of the negative messages and comments came through Facebook, I was one click away from the senders' personal information, photos, and posts. Did they know that? Were they aware that when they called me a *libtard* I could also see the name of the high school where they taught English? That when they told me how I should die that I was just three pages away from finding out their aunt's favorite band? Sending hate on social media, especially Facebook, was like sending a hate letter via snail mail and paper-clipping every photo ever taken of you, your employer's address, and a partial family tree. And it was this information that I used to construct a full three-dimensional backstory for each of my HATE FOLDER occupants.

Using the available information as support beams, I would project intricate narratives onto the biographical gaps in their profile. If someone, for example, had one picture of a family reunion, and another photo of a car they recently restored by hand, I would connect the two photos in my mind by imagining them driving that refurbished car to that family reunion. I would see them arriving to joyous cheers from all of their cousins who had been "liking" updates about the renovation along the way. "You finally did it!" one uncle, who was tagged in a recent post, would exclaim. This hypothetical montage helped soften the image of a person who might have told me that I had a punchable face.

By fashioning a Frankenstein monster out of the disparate details left in my detractors' ever-growing digital trails, I was able to paint vivid scenes from their lives—tiny moments of fictionalized mundanity—and it was these scenes that kept me sane. By imagining the most loving backstories I could, I was able to convince myself that they were human beings with feelings, which made me less scared.

And so, that is why I find myself standing here, outside my boss's office, scrolling through the profile of a stranger named Josh.

III. PAUSE

I make my way back to my desk where I slump into my rolling chair and pull up Josh's profile on my computer. I've lost track of how many times I've reread his message, but by now I've practically memorized it: "Youre a moron. Youre the reason this country is dividing itself. All your videos are meerly opinion, and an awful opinion i must say. Just stop. Plus, being Gay is a sin." *Meerly*, I whisper back to myself, hoping that identifying this typo will somehow offset the sting of his message. It doesn't.

There is something different about Josh, though. Whereas other HATE FOLDER members have scattered biographical data, forcing me to do more work to fill in the blanks, Josh posts so frequently that there is little I need to fictionalize. Now I am no longer constructing an imaginary human being, but simply paying attention to the one right here in front of me.

I see, for example, that he has shared a meme that shows Hillary Clinton mesmerized by the falling confetti at the DNC beneath text that reads "IS THAT CONFETTI OR 30000 SHREDDED EMAILS?"

Another scroll reveals a paraphrased Bible passage he recently shared that says, "Do not be deceived. Neither . . . homosexuals, nor sodomites . . . will inherit the kingdom of God."

In one post, though, he is raising money for his high school theater production.

In another he is posing with a birthday cake.

"Celebratory lunch made by me," he had captioned a picture of a meal he prepared. A comment on his post tells me that he had been cast in his school's musical.

A third post is a geotag at a movie theater where he apparently saw the Pixar movie *Finding Dory*. "What a tearjerker. LOVED IT!" he wrote. Todd and I had gone to see the movie that summer and we, too, cried throughout it.

There is a kindness to him, a sweet vulnerability. He seems to boldly resist the anti-earnest edicts of the internet and shares exactly what he is feeling, right as he feels it.

"Anyone want to hang out tonight? Don't want to spend my Friday night sitting on my bed watching TV," he wrote in a post. I think back to the many Friday nights I spent inside, waiting for an invitation to a hangout that never came.

"Feeling alone," he confessed in another post. I suspect if I had kept a digital record of every thought I had when I was a teenager that I would have written something almost identical.

I tap my phone to check the time and see that I've spent the entire afternoon on Josh's profile. This was another frustrating thing about the hate: the sheer amount of time it stole from me. I have a comedy show in a couple hours and I don't have any material prepared.

Since I'm not a stand-up comedian, I usually have to find a creative way to fit into a lineup of traditional comics. Sometimes I'll read aloud an essay I've written, other times I program an automated robot voice to lead the audience in a dance party, but those require significant preparation and time that I don't have. I entertain the thought of pulling out at the last minute, but I don't want to do that to my friend Nicole who is the producer of tonight's show. I need to come up with an idea quickly.

This performance won't be released as a video, which means that it won't be seen by millions of people. Instead, it will be seen by the dozen or so audience members who are down to go to a comedy show at 11:00 P.M. on a weeknight. No matter what I do tonight I won't be able to unlock a level in the game. There will be no points to collect. Strangely, this is motivating. A hint of creative freedom and a warm nostalgia come over me as I recall writing short plays for the audiences of the New York Neo-Futurists. I didn't have the luxury of that speed anymore. Back then I would take time to consider what was on my mind, how it affected me, and then create from there. It's pretty clear what's on my mind right now. I look at Josh's profile and then his message and then back to his profile. I double click on the HATE FOLDER and scroll through its growing population. Then, tapping me on the shoulder like an old friend is a question: *What am I going to do about it?*

I've been seeing stories of internet harassers getting fired. This always seems like justice on the surface, but it leaves a weird taste in my mouth. Does causing the harasser to lose their job make the sting of harassment go away for the victim? And does this job loss actually stop the person from doing it again? Maybe. I don't know. But time is running out and I'll need to leave soon for the show, so I need to work fast.

I click back on Josh's profile. "Works at Best Buy," his profile reads. This sits just beneath the town he lives in, and one tab away from a quick Google search that can show me exactly which Best Buy location employs him.

Finally, I have an idea.

◎

"Hello!" I greet the audience as I make my way to a laptop that has been set for me on the other side of the stage. After introducing myself, I open with a question to the crowd: What do you get when you express opinions on the internet? I click on the forward arrow of the laptop's keyboard and the next slide appears. "Trolls!" I shout, as a photo of looming ogres flashes on the screen behind me. There are scattered nods of recognition throughout the room.

Okay, I think, *we're off to a good start.* I click forward to begin navigating through screenshots I've pulled from the HATE FOLDER, reading them aloud as I go.

"'If AIDS had a voice . . . and a stupid haircut . . .'" I recite from a comment, then telling the crowd that I'd be honored to be the voice of AIDS, but "I also get my haircut from my husband so go fuck yourself." The audience cheers. *Click.*

A screenshot appears that just reads "'gaywad fagggggg.'" I read aloud this two-word message from a person named Donovan, over-emphasizing the five extra *g*'s that he has thrown in there. The audience giggles. *Click.*

Josh's message is seen on the screen and I read it to them, identifying his missing apostrophes, misspelled words, and his decision to capitalize the *g* in *Gay.* The audience bursts with laughter when I point this out. *Click.*

"'Fucking faggot ass, go ride with a cop and pull someone over in the hood and be the first guy to approach the drivers window PUSSY.'" I dramatically reperform this message from a man named Kevin, hitting the *P* of his final all-caps word. *Click.*

As the slideshow continues, I keep calling out every typo, every "there" that should be a "their," every run-on sentence, and every piece of faulty logic. The audience is loving it way more than I thought they would, and I am loving that they are loving it.

"'Were you born a bitch or did you just learn to be one over time? You're such a faggot,'" I recite from a message written by someone named Brian. I point out that Brian's finger must have slipped because his immediate follow-up to this message was the thumbs-up emoji and the audience delights at this gaffe. There is something unexpectedly therapeutic about externalizing the HATE FOLDER into a slideshow. It's as if I'm taking the arrows that have been shot my way and repurposing them into entertainment. *Click.*

"Trolls suck, right?!!" I ask the audience like we're at a rally.

"Yes!" they dutifully shout in response. *Click.*

I start to switch gears. "So, I started exploring Josh's Facebook." *Click.*

Josh's message reappears on the screen to remind them. *Click.*

The anti-Hillary meme is shown. The audience is silent. *Click.*

The Bible quote condemning homosexuality comes next.

"But then . . ." I tease. *Click.*

Now, on the projection screen is Josh's confession about crying while watching *Finding Dory*. The audience erupts with laughter and cheers. *Click.*

Josh's post that says "Anyone wanna talk? Im bored" is now on the screen. There is a sudden shift. Many let out tender aws. *Click.*

"Feeling alone," Josh's next post reads. The room has now completely shifted to be on Josh's side. I take a beat to acknowledge the change, and then keep going. *Click.*

"Now Josh doesn't realize that I have full access to everything on Facebook even though we're not friends because he messaged me," I begin, leading the audience around our twist. "So here's what he didn't realize he included on his profile." *Click.*

"He works at Best Buy," I identify. "So I looked up that Best Buy." *Click.*

The next slide displays the number for that Best Buy location. I pull out my phone, and a few audience members gasp, sure that they know where this is going. I punch in the number, put it on speakerphone, and hold it up to the microphone.

"Thanks for calling Best Buy," the prerecorded voice on the other end of the phone says. "We're currently closed."

I press *0* to get an operator. "Thanks for calling Best Buy. We're currently closed." In my rush to prepare this slideshow I had failed to test out whether or not they were open or even had a voicemail at all.

"So the next part of my bit will not work," I say to the audience, slightly embarrassed. "But what I was planning is that we were going to leave a voicemail on Best Buy's voicemail that went like this." I click the next slide, which I had intended for the audience to read aloud into Best Buy's answering machine, and they kindly play along and read it in unison:

"Hi, we are sending love to your employee Josh! He's a good person. Please ask him to pay it forward by expressing appreciation to someone he may disagree with."

I thank the audience and say good night. They cheer as I step off the stage, triumphant. It's a different triumph than the one that comes from a coin haul of likes and shares. It's something else. Something calmer, more whole. This was a sort of homecoming for me. By returning to my more earnest, sincere self I was tapping into something more authentic.

Tomorrow I will return to the game. I will continue sprinting at the speed of trending topics, responding to the news as it happens. I will don my avatar's snarky costume and stare into a camera lens to boldly slay whatever new Goliaths may present themselves. But that's tomorrow. Tonight I revel in this contentment and, just like old times, I take the late train home, soaring through the tunnels beneath the city, knowing that I just made a connection with a few dozen people.

IV. WINNING

As October rolls along, the challenges keep coming and I'm ready to tackle them head-on. As lovely as it was to return to my softer, more sincere voice with the slideshow, I'm focused on domination. With the November presidential election on the horizon there is a Big Boss to slay and I need to do everything I can to fight back. Luckily, I'm getting better. My writing is tightening, my takes are sharpening, and I'm getting quicker and quicker at my responses. I'm even becoming a better reader of the internet, a stronger interpreter of its ever-evolving trending topics, like one of those veteran stock analysts who can predict a crash months before it happens. The news cycle continues to be an unwieldy mechanical bull and I am staying on for longer and longer. The speed with which I develop a take on a news story is getting faster, too.

Most important though, each video I make is getting more and more views. With every like, follow, and share, I believe I am educating the masses, resisting the conservative agenda, and bringing my growing audience over to the right side of history with crisp jokes and watchable content. Writing in my avatar's voice becomes so second nature that it is no longer a costume, but skin. His voice is now my voice. I have perfected the epic takedown, proudly beating the battle drum of justice to the intoxicating cheers of many.

With each new milestone I hear the dopamine-inducing sound of a coin hitting a pile of other coins, like the synthetic chime of a slot machine. Three videos in a row with over one million views, *ching*. Thirty thousand likes on my Facebook page, *ching*. Over a thousand likes on a joke, *ching*. A nomination for a prestigious award, *ching ching*. And then, I finally hit the motherlode, the crowning achievement of internet hierarchy: the verified blue check mark. This circular blue emblem appears on my Facebook, Twitter, and Instagram profiles right beside my name like a cerulean crown that finally bestows upon me the status I have long pined for. *New level: unlocked.*

But as the coins pile up, the HATE FOLDER is growing larger, too. My haters are saying much more violent things, which now make other messages seem lighter by comparison. Josh's message, which stung when I first received it, was now in the same folder as "how bout I dress like your mom and go sucks some cock just like her" and "your father should've beaten you more." This makes me cherish my coins all the more closely as they are now the counterweight to each piece of hate I receive, but I try to take it in stride. As October flips to November, I am certain that all of this is worth it, that I am enduring the hate for a much greater cause, and we will reap the benefits on Tuesday, November 8.

V. LOSING

Election week finally arrives.

Sunday. My computer chimes with an email from my boss Ethan.

"I'm sorry that you're going through all of this," his email begins. "I wish there were an easy answer. You are the face of something that certain people don't want to hear. I'm guessing, from the way they react, that they feel like they're being attacked personally, so they attack personally. I wonder if there's a way where you can start a dialogue."

Since our conversation in his office, he's been actively checking in on me. There is no rule book for what a boss should do when their employee gets a swarm of harassment on the internet. It is too new a problem to have a precedent, so here he is doing his best to form one.

Tuesday. The day has finally arrived and I post my way through it.

I cast my vote with my mom and take a selfie with her to show off our stickers. *Refresh. Refresh. Refresh.* 1,065 likes. *Ching.*

As I rehearse for our Election Night livestream, I scroll Twitter and discover that Donald Trump and I voted at the same polling place. A gift from the gods of content. "Trump & I share a polling place. Our votes will count equally. Proud to say that they'll cancel each other out. Democracy is cool," I tweet. I screenshot it and share it on Instagram and Facebook. *Refresh. Refresh. Refresh.* 1,800 likes. *Ching.*

Early returns begin trickling in and Texas is prematurely shaded blue. "Texas, blue looks good on you. I say buy it. #ElectionNight." I tweet it out. *Refresh. Refresh. Refresh.* 490 likes. *Ching.*

I tally up all of the likes I've received as if they are official returns. *We're going to win*, I think, taking my social media engagement as a bellwether for our national election. But as the evening progresses, the unthinkable begins to happen: Donald Trump pulls ahead. My tweet from hours earlier has not aged well. Confusion and distress set in around me, but rather than talking to those in my physical vicinity, I walk up to my digital podium and offer a calming tone of assurance to the countless people I am sure are eagerly awaiting my statement. "No matter who wins, remember folks: the work starts tomorrow." I screenshot it and share it on Instagram and Facebook. *Refresh. Refresh. Refresh.* 1,497 likes. *Ching.*

Wednesday Early Hours. At 2:29 A.M. (EST), Donald Trump is declared the winner of the 2016 presidential election.

"What happened?" my cabdriver asks me as I crawl into his back seat, exhausted and depressed.

"He won," I say, somberly.

"Oh," he replies, matching my tone. We sit in silence for the rest of the ride.

I open Twitter, and my thumbs hover over the keyboard as we glide across the Manhattan Bridge but I can't seem to think of anything to say. No likes. In place of the synthetic coin chime is a hollow silence and the droning hum of the taxi's engine.

Wednesday Morning. Waking up, I am still blindsided that this long-shot outcome is now our new reality. How had we not seen this coming? Unthinkingly, I open the HATE FOLDER and mindlessly scroll through the screenshots. I click on one and then hold my finger down on an arrow that causes the messages and comments to cascade like a flip-book. I see flashes of the backstories I had constructed for each of their authors. The refurbished cars, the family reunions, the schools, the friend groups.

Maybe, I think, this folder is a better representation of the country than I had previously thought. Most of them probably voted for him. When I consider them as a collective, I am angry and hurt, but when I think of them as individuals, whose scattered biographical details I've woven into novellas, I see that they are simply human beings, whose lives are just very different from mine. My mind jumps back and forth between these two truths—understanding them, on the one hand, as a terrifying army of Trump supporters, and, on the other hand, individual people subject to influence and power just like me. Will that help? I'm not sure.

Friday. I take the day off so I can surprise Todd up at law school. I sit slouched in my seat on the Amtrak, staring out the window as I watch the late New England fall fly by. As the train pulls toward Boston, the trees are growing more and more bare but I have no more clarity than I did before. Instead, a random memory keeps coming to me.

In middle school my dad took me on a long-planned, highly anticipated trip to Los Angeles so that we could tour the movie studios. Tour after tour, we learned the tricks of filmmaking from the enthusiastic tour guides who led us around. On-camera rain, we were told, was actually a mixture of water and milk. Water didn't show up well on screen. Sometimes it took a whole day to film just one page of a script. The exterior of a character's house might be miles away from the interior set of that same home. But today there is one filmmaking trick that feels especially apt.

To give the illusion that a scene is taking place in the middle of a massive crowd, like, say, a protest, a director wouldn't need twenty thousand extras for the shot. They wouldn't even need CGI. All they needed to do was pack a few dozen people very tightly into the frame and viewers' minds would fill in the rest. By seeing a shot of twenty extras packed shoulder to shoulder, all carrying protest signs, our minds just assume that there is a sea of people surrounding them. Wasn't the internet doing the same thing? Wasn't I tricked into believing that one thousand likes was the whole world? All this time I'd been operating under the illusion that I was having a dialogue with *everyone* when, in fact, I was just monologuing at *some*.

Perhaps activism through explainer video isn't really activism at all if that video only reaches people who already agree with me. It's humbling to realize that I'm not nearly as influential as I think I am. The audience I had believed I was addressing in every video, tweet, and photo was more of a closed room than an endless auditorium. The conversations I thought I was starting were just between people who already agreed with me. On the internet, as in Hollywood, something small can look massive when shown from the right angle. A few dozen extras crammed into a well-designed frame can fool us into believing they are surrounded by a sea of people, just like thirty thousand followers and two hundred shares can seem like the whole world. What was the point of the game now that I was seeing the scale accurately? What were these coins actually worth?

My videos alone were never going to sufficiently evangelize progressive ideas. If I indeed wanted to involve more people in the conversation—people who didn't yet see the problem with any of the issues I frequently discussed, like, say, policing, or transphobia, or microaggressions—was I succeeding, or was I simply enjoying the reverberations of virality in my own little echo chamber, thinking that I was slaying Goliath when I was simply cosplaying battle reenactments with my fellow self-identified Davids?

I don't even know if I'm worthy of the "activist" title some have bestowed upon me. All this time I had been determining which issues to cover based on what was being most talked about on the internet. Did that make me an activist or just another player riding the wave of a trending topic in pursuit of a coin haul? In trading nuance for easy coins, complexity for simplicity, was I the social justice advocate I thought I was, or was I simply playing one online?

My avatar had become a caricature of me, so binary in his thinking, so simplistic in his pronouncements, that he was unrecognizable from the real me. Yet he had gotten so popular that he was almost out of my control. His costume had fused to my skin simply because I wore it for too long. I thought that his biting tone and crisp takedowns would cut through the noise of the internet, but now I see that he and I were only adding to it.

What is my work going to look like now? Before it had so clearly been the battle cry of a winning army, but what would it sound like when we were down? Truly, I have no idea, so I open up my Notes app and write down whatever half-baked ideas come to mind.

A line from Ethan's email replays in my head. *I wonder if there's a way where you can start a dialogue.* I think of the term *common ground* that seems to be floating around the zeitgeist and write that down, imagining some sort of lighthearted web series where I play games with Trump supporters and see what we have in common, although that seems pretty one-note. I then begin to imagine a live touring show where I speak to Republicans and members of homophobic churches.

People who hate me, my thumbs type into my Notes app. That's about as far as my creative mind is willing to take me today.

Saturday. Figuring that I need to start somewhere, I call Matt, my most conservative friend. And when I say that Matt is my most conservative friend, I mean that he is a registered independent who has, on occasion, voted for Republican candidates.

"Dylannnnn," he says as he answers my call, tenderly elongating the *n*'s as he has since freshman year of college.

Matt and I last spoke almost a year ago when the primaries were still in full swing. Over beers he told Todd and me that he would never, under any circumstances, cast a vote for Hillary Clinton, and I am hopeful that he can offer a glimmer of insight into why he decided to vote for Trump.

"Are you kidding me? Of course I didn't vote for him," he replies in shock that I even asked. My relief is offset by disappointment, as I had hoped that he could make sense of all of this and, in the process, help me believe that my ideological network was wider than the thin hallway it seemed to be.

As we say our goodbyes, it occurs to me that this is one of the few conversations I've had about politics away from the game and not in front of an audience. I like this feeling.

Soon after we hang up, I see that my Facebook page has a new message.

"Hey brother. I'm a Trump supporter. I have watched your videos and was wondering if you would be willing to talk? I think a discussion without yelling or screaming at each other could really maybe be beneficial for us both."

Something seems to be in the air, and I begin to fantasize about inviting this man into the studios for an interview, but there is little information that is publicly accessible on his profile and fear takes over me. *What if this is a setup?* Perhaps this idea of speaking to the other side is only a fantasy.

Sunday. On the train ride back down to New York City, I think about how nice it was to talk to Matt, but how scared I was to further engage with the Trump supporter who messaged me. How will I ever be able to speak to "the other side" if I don't have access to anyone who is part of it and am too scared to speak to strangers who reach out to me? I try thinking of any Trump supporters in my life who I would want to talk to, but my mind is blank.

VI. A GLITCH

I continue to make videos for the two months that follow the election, collecting points along the way and adding to my ever-growing HATE FOLDER. Part of me still wants to change course, but why fix something that isn't broken? The coins keep accruing and what I'm doing seems to be working just fine.

It is December 30, and tonight I have another show. This time it's my friend Josh's and I reconsult his invitation email to figure out what I'm going to do. "We're gonna have comics give a presentation or talk about something *good* that happened this year. Like a Positive Year In Review. 5-7 minutes. Ya down??? Luv, J."

Something good, I think to myself, scanning my arsenal for what might fit the bill for this show. But every idea I have seems to always return to Josh. The other Josh. HATE FOLDER Josh. This seems like the perfect opportunity to do that slideshow one last time, which means that this time I will need to actually reach a Best Buy employee. And if this is indeed its final performance, I figure I should film it.

In preparation for the slideshow's social media debut, I carefully comb the deck, redacting last names, hiding personal information, and blurring any faces that may appear, but I decide to leave in the detail that Josh works at Best Buy, confident that disclosing his employment at a company with 125,000 employees nationwide won't be revealing too much. I engineer a way to actually reach the manager of this Best Buy, which involves the genius move of calling them when they are actually open.

"Thank you for calling Best Buy!" a voice answers in the middle of the day.

"Oh, hey," I stammer, taken slightly aback that I am finally talking to a real live human voice. I make sure that I'm recording so that I can play this at tonight's show. "Um, I just wanted to leave just a random message for one of your employees. Um, I think their name is Josh? Um, I just wanted you to, uh, let him know that he helped me the other day in the store and that he's just a great person and I hope he keeps being great to people."

"I am so happy to hear that, sir," the employee says.

Now that I've finally reached the store, I am overcome with a strangely bittersweet feeling. This will be the last time that I make this phone call and I find myself preemptively missing someone I don't even know, a person who called me a "moron" and reminded me that my sexuality was a "sin."

I do the show, and the slideshow hits exactly as it did before, getting laughs where I want them, gasps when I need them, and adoring coos as I navigate Josh's profile. On January 2, I upload the video to Facebook and YouTube.

"Empathy for My Trolls," I type into the video's title field. *Publish.*

So long, Josh, I think. *I wish I could see your face when your manager delivers this message.*

Late that evening, my phone pings with a notification. "Your page has a new message." Like a good user, I click to open it.

"Do you really think that going throgh my facebook and showing off the posts when i was depressed is a good idea? When you're trying to promote peace and love? All it does is show that you're a hypocrite."

I freeze. It's Josh.

How could he have seen the video? I think. And then, in shock at my own shock. *Of course he saw the video! How could I think he wouldn't?*

I have stumbled upon a glitch of the game, a loophole that the game's architects didn't foresee. All this time I had forgotten that Josh was a living, breathing human being with feelings, even while sharing a slideshow designed to show that Josh was a living, breathing human being with feelings. So distracted by performing "empathy for my trolls," I forgot to actually have it. But hadn't he, in sending me his first message, forgotten *I* was a living, breathing human being with feelings, too? Hadn't the concept of my humanity also escaped *him*?

And through this glitch, I finally see something I hadn't before. Everything I was wrestling with after the election is now crystalizing right in front of me: The internet distorts reality. Not just for me, but for all of us.

We think we are seeing others clearly, but we aren't. The sheer volume of people that we pass every day forces us to turn everyone we encounter into the simplest version of themselves: a profile picture and whatever identifiers we can see in their bios.

We think we know who we're seeing online, but we don't, really. We can't see the life lived beyond the profile pictures, no matter how long we spend imagining that life.

We think we are showing ourselves clearly, but we aren't. We are able to seem more famous than we actually are, more aggressive than we mean to be, more unbothered than we truly feel. The internet turns us into caricatures of ourselves, thin drawings that overemphasize some features but conceal all the rest.

We think we're seeing everything when we aren't. Much of what we see is dictated by the mysterious algorithms that feed us what *they* think we want to see, which itself is based on a complicated arithmetic of what we've engaged with and what powerful entities want us to see.

We think we are seeing everyone, but we're just seeing a trick crowd shot on a Hollywood soundstage. A small number of people smashed into a frame, causing our minds to fill in the rest.

I thought that by playing the game I was cutting through the distortion, when in fact I was helping to amplify it. Each rule I had obediently followed contributed to the warp of the internet. By obsessively following the trending topics, I was contributing to a sense of groupthink. By creating these tiny nuggets of videos, I was often removing necessary context, shaving it down to its most basic and shareable form. By adopting a more aggressive, snide voice I was constructing a false self, a meaner avatar who concealed my own authentic voice. By seeing those I disagreed with as my "opponents," I was distilling them to their most basic qualities, and worse: I was pushing them away from the very topics I wanted to discuss with them. And in my constant commentary, I was never really listening, just contributing to the noise in the echoing hall of podiums. All of this helped perpetuate a binary, overly simplistic worldview that stripped the conversation—and each other—of nuance and complexity. We were no longer individuals but holograms that we sent off to battle for fake points that we could never really cash in.

The internet, I am now learning, is not built to mitigate conflict; in fact, it seems like it's built to sustain it. I had so deeply bought into the game, thinking that winning would start a conversation. But it was the game itself, and my allegiance to it, that obscured the humanity of the people I was playing against. It obscured my own humanity, too. Without realizing it, I had hurt someone who once hurt me. I had become the Goliath.

So, I ask myself. *What am I going to do about it?*

2

conversation is a dance

No no no no no no no. This is all my mind can say at the moment.

My fingers tremble over my laptop's keyboard, waiting in position for a directive while their command center has been thrown into a state of chaos.

Go away! I think. *You're not supposed to see me!*

In the absence of any coherent guidance from my brain, my fingers decide to take action themselves.

"Hey Josh," they type, clacking on the keys.

Seconds later, Josh's typing bubbles appear. I watch the three dots jump up and down, in smooth, synchronized motion as if they are the opening act of his next message, hyping up the crowd for what's to come. My heart thumps in my chest. Finally, the bubbles fade away and his message takes the stage.

"Hello Dylan. How are you?"

Should I answer honestly? Should I tell him that I'm currently having a minor panic attack because a person who was once safely contained in my HATE FOLDER has just reemerged in my inbox? Should I tell him that I had no expectation that he'd ever see the video even though I had made it public on the internet? Thankfully, my fingers take the lead once again.

"I'm good - it's actually very nice to hear from you." *Send.*

"I'm surprise to hear from you, but glad." *Send.*

I notice the typo but move on.

"Are you hurt by the video?" *Send.*

"Because that was absolutely not my intention." *Send.*

The typing bubbles reappear, mocking me with their somersaults.

"I appreciate that," he writes back. "Im glad to hear back from you. I wanted to talk about the video. Not so much hurt as embarrassed."

"Even though I made sure to make it anonymous?" I ask, now worrying that I accidentally forgot to blur some personal detail of his.

"I know it wasn't and i respect what you do."

I try to decode this. *What does he mean? He knows it wasn't* what*? He knows it wasn't anonymous? That makes no sense.* Then I look back in the messages and see that he's responding to my earlier point that it wasn't my intention to hurt him.

"And it wasn't exactly anonymous," Josh continues. "I got this video in my inbox from someone. So, somebody found out it was me, and messaged me. Whos to say theres not more who found out?"

"Would you prefer that I take it down?" I ask, offering the only remedy that comes to mind.

"Tbh, I don't know. You made some valid points in there and you did make me open my eyes. I just dont want more messages like the one i got. It was very hateful."

A pang of guilt takes residence in my chest. Because of my video about hate messages, Josh is now apparently receiving hate messages himself. Online hate: It's the gift that keeps on giving.

"You shouldn't be getting hateful messages," I say. "I truly didn't think anyone would know it was you." Then, circling back to my offer to take the video down: "You can also take your time with answering that."

"Answering what?" he asks, confused.

We are out of sync, typing so quickly that the answer to one question comes after the next question has already been asked.

"Whether or not you want me to take the video down," I explain. "I'll leave it up to you and will honor whatever you want to do." My fingers fumble as they type, gradually regaining contact with my brain.

"Can i make a suggestion?" he asks, but I barrel on, still focused on the topic of the hate he received.

"Ironically, as you can tell from the video, i get a lot of harassment. And i don't want you to be getting any of it. It sucks," I say, and then, noticing that he has a suggestion, I reply, "Please make a suggestion: happy to hear it."

"I can," he says.

He "can" what? He can . . . make a suggestion?

"I feel extremely bad for what I said. I was in the wrong." I now understand that he's saying he can tell from the video that I get a lot of harassment. This message exchange needs a live decoder.

"I hope you don't feel too bad," I offer. "If you're apologizing I completely accept it." Trying to rectify our increasingly crossed wires, I bring it back to the topic at hand: "(open for your suggestion)."

His typing bubbles appear. *What is his suggestion? Is he going to ask me to call back Best Buy? Was my employee review not thorough enough? Was he fired?*

"Instead of taking down the video, i was wondering if you would consider making another video with me (via skype) that way i have a chance to say what i feel i need to say."

"100%," I type instinctively. I don't think through how, or when, or where, but I just say yes. It's as if my half-baked concept for a dialogue show in the aftershock of the 2016 presidential election, the vague sketch I had of speaking to people from "the other side," is now actualizing right before my eyes.

"And yes," he begins. *Yes to what?* "Im so sorry for what i said. Youre a great guy." *Oh, right. He's confirming that he's apologizing. This is sweet.*

He types another message: "Really?" This message thread is now officially an advanced level puzzle.

"You're a great guy too Josh," I say, referring to his first point. And then, to address his second: "Yes, really."

"When would you wanna do it?" he asks.

"I think we should do it this week." My mind has been well trained to swoop in on every video opportunity possible, so I want to film this as quickly as I can.

"That would be cool with me. And yeah, any time after 5 (I have musical rehrsal)." I want to say *I know you have musical rehearsal*, but I think better of it.

"Before the video," he asks, "would it be possible, either skype or by phone, talk to you. I dont wanna just go into a video without talking to you first."

"Hahhaha of course," I say. "The videos I make for work, I always talk to my guests first."

Before we decide on a time, Josh asks, "So, out of all your hate comments, what made mine stick out?"

"I usually always check out and see who is messaging me, cuz sometimes the messages get pretty scary," I say, recognizing how surreal it is to invite a person from the HATE FOLDER into my HATE FOLDER coping mechanism. "But when you had messaged me I noticed you were in the school musical (like I was) and I remember thinking 'oh, but this kid is so cool and so nice.'"

"What made you choose the post on my page that you did?" Josh asks, referring to the posts that closed out the slideshow, the posts where he put out feelers for plans, checked in at movie theaters, and confessed to loneliness.

"Those were the posts that reminded me of me. They showed that you were a real & good person who felt real things."

"I do have to say, finding dory is a tearjerker though," he says.

"JOSH I CRIED MY EYES OUT IN THAT MOVIE. It was truly, like, that post that i was like we're actually similar."

"So," Josh says. "What time tomorrow?"

◎

It's 5:55 P.M. *Five more minutes.* I have been patiently waiting for the last of my coworkers to leave while eyeing the digital clock on my computer monitor. On a ripped piece of notebook paper in front of me is Josh's phone number, hastily scribbled down in Sharpie just in case I accidentally deleted his messages.

"See you tomorrow!" I say to the last straggler, my voice straining to hide my nerves. I haven't told anyone other than Todd about this call with Josh. I'm scared, unsure of who he might be offline, but I'm also excited, hopeful about where this might lead. Ever since the election I've been consciously reconsidering the approach I take with my work and the voice I speak with publicly. I have always wanted to reach people who disagree with me; I just haven't yet figured out how. Perhaps this is the first step.

5:59 P.M.

I get up from my desk and head toward the small conference room that I've reserved for this call. I hug the walls as I go like some sort of action star in a climactic, high-octane scene where they are scaling a skyscraper to escape a vengeful helicopter. Of course, I'm not on a mission to save the world from a plutonium explosion. I'm just on my way to make a phone call.

Dylan, chill.

Finally, I reach my destination: a small alcove that sits across from the studio where I film my videos, the very videos that Josh thinks are "meerly opinion."

As I settle into the plush couch, a wave of worry comes over me. *Am I about to be duped? Is Josh who he says he is?* And then, a new thought: *Is he even real?* The idea of bots is just beginning to enter the public lexicon. Now my mind runs wild with the thought that Josh isn't a human being at all and is instead a complex line of code, expertly programmed to seem like a human being, complete with typos and the illusion of feelings. But fear is what kept me from having a conversation with that Trump supporter, the one who messaged me after the election, and if I want to venture outside of my echo chamber, then I can't let that same fear hold me back today.

Once again I enlist my fingers to punch in the first three digits of his number—an area code that I've never dialed, representing a town I've never been to. I tap in the rest of his number and wait.

Ring. My heart thumps in my throat.

Ring. I notice the paper with his number is crumpled in my sweaty hands.

Ri—

"Hello?" answers a voice on the other end of the line. It's a deeper voice than I was expecting for a high school senior.

"Hi, is this Josh?" I ask, wondering if maybe I got the wrong number.

"Yes, sir," the voice says back.

"Oh, hi—great. Hi, Josh. Um, well this is Dylan Marron. Is this, um, is this still a good time for you. Or, like, does it still work to talk now?"

"Yes, sir," Josh says. I've only heard him say two words, three if we count his opening hello, but I already sense a calm maturity in his voice.

A brief moment of silence hangs in the air. *It's your turn*, the silence says to me. But I have no idea what to say so I pretend like this is a normal conversation, a mundane catchup between friends.

"How's your day so far?" I ask, as if talking to Josh after school is our routine, and here I am, mindlessly fixing him a snack before he starts his homework. I wince at the thought that I've overstepped.

"It's going okay."

"Good," I say. "I'm happy to be talking to you."

Slowly, we ease into the chat now that our voices have sniffed each other out with small talk. We discuss his high school musical, and I share that I was in my high school theater productions, too. I confess that the musical was always tricky for me, given that I had little musical talent at all, but I share that what I lacked in singing talent I made up for with unearned confidence and intermediate tap skills. We reestablish that *Finding Dory* was, in fact, a tearjerker and I share again that Todd and I cried in the theater when we saw it, too.

We're not really covering new ground. We revisit what we discussed last night on Facebook Messenger. But now instead of our keyboards, we're using our voices and because of this I hear his every pause, which tells me far more than the anxiety-inducing typing bubbles ever did. I sense when he's nervous and when he's confident. His Southern accent transports me to his hometown, his elongated vowels an immediate flight to his region. His cadence—slow and deliberate—is distinctly his own and exists in stark contrast to my more hurried and nervous speech pattern. His words recline while mine scamper. Now we catch each other's *ums* and *uhs* and stutters, which had previously been concealed by a simple stroke of the backspace key. Best of all, we are no longer caught up in the jumbled queue of misaligned questions and answers. Now we are finding a rhythm together.

Hearing Josh's voice finally allows me to picture him more clearly, and with this clearer image, he is no longer the distant enemy but, in a weird way, a new friend. Is the human voice the missing component in the fictional backstories I've been weaving for the HATE FOLDER tenants? Is this what can connect a two-year-old profile picture and a series of posts?

As we talk more, I remember reading once about a study conducted by a biological anthropologist named Leslie Seltzer who found that phone calls and hugs had the same effect on levels of cortisol, the stress hormone. Additionally, Seltzer's research showed that both a hug and a phone call released the "love hormone" oxytocin. Of course, Seltzer conducted this test on a group of preteen girls and their mothers. But now that I'm on the phone with Josh, it is as if we are submitting a new group to Seltzer's study. That, however anecdotal, the same holds true for one-time internet enemies.

"Do you like high school?" I ask.

"Am I allowed to curse?" he asks back.

At first I think this is a joke, but when he doesn't laugh I realize that he is genuinely asking for my permission. "Yes," I say.

"It's hell," he says with a deflated sadness—something I would have never heard in a text-based message exchange.

"Huh," I say, instinctively trying to fill the silence.

"I get picked on a lot," Josh confesses after a beat.

"I know what that's like," I tell him, prompting a vivid flashback to the older boy who threw a book at my head in Spanish class while I was taking notes, his cheeks blown out to suppress a laugh when I looked back to see who threw it, his palm low-fiving the friend beside him for successfully hitting their intended target. I bring myself back to Josh.

There is a brief silence and I take this opportunity to address the last line in Josh's message: "So, you think being gay is a sin?"

"Yeah," he says. "I believe what I said, but it's not the Christian way to say it. And I'm sorry that it hurt."

What do I say in response? If I were the version of myself that I play in my videos, Avatar Dylan, I would mercilessly rip into this idea. I would say some bold, well-written clapback that would absolutely eviscerate both Josh and this homophobic talking point. But I am not staring down the barrel of a camera lens, speaking to my many fans. I am speaking into a phone receiver that goes directly to Josh, the person who just said the thing that I would want to eviscerate. He is no longer an abstract concept, nor a representative of all conservatism or homophobia or archaic Christianity, but an individual person who has been taught these things.

There is no audience here. There is no recording. This is an exclusive performance just for us. I am not my popular and snarky avatar, nor is he the profile picture that called me a moron. Now he is a live voice, a voice that has just told me about being bullied in high school—a voice that reminds me of my own. These similarities don't excuse what he said, but now I cannot unsee his humanity. All these facts about him—who he is and what he has experienced and, yes, also what he said to me—must all be taken together.

What do I say in response?

"Oh." I say. And then: "Well, thanks for saying that." And then, "My husband went to seminary. For a while he was thinking of being a minister. There's a whole community of people who are Christian and queer."

"Like I said, it's what I believe."

"Yeah," I say back, gently. Avatar Dylan is somewhere in a digital video box fuming that I'm not pummeling Josh back in response.

"Hey, before I forget," I say, changing direction. "Did your boss at Best Buy ever give you my message?"

Josh chuckles, then sighs. "You know, the truth is, I don't even work at Best Buy. I just thought it was a cool store when I made my profile."

"What?!" I say with a laugh, now thinking of the poor manager scratching their head after they hung up.

This conversation has surprised me. I want to take this to the next level: I want to speak to Josh face-to-face. I want to turn this into a video. Less for the points that I might accrue, and more because I genuinely want other people to see what is happening right now, to see that this isn't so terrifying, and that there is something actually hopeful about this phone call. Last night, when Josh suggested making a video in our Facebook message exchange I instinctively agreed but couldn't quite picture how it would go. Now I finally can see it.

"Josh," I begin, "do you still want to make that video?"

◎

"Hi, I'm Dylan Marron and today I am going to be shutting down bullshit with a guy who trolled me." I am looking directly into the camera. The hot lights of the recording studio beat down on me. Dustin, my collaborator at Seriously.TV, silently stands behind the camera, his eyes fixed on the color levels in the camera's monitor. Alison, our production assistant, sits at attention on the studio's couch to ensure everything goes smoothly.

It is March of 2017, more than two months since Josh and I first spoke to each other on the phone. He and I had initially planned to record this video a few days after our call, but as I was prepping production, he got cold feet. "Could we maybe hold off on doing the vid for a week or 2. I wanna consider all angles," he messaged me when the studio had already been booked. Worried that my enthusiasm had turned him off, I gave him some space until he was ready, and when he was months later, I got right to work.

Aside from the normal production logistics, I needed to figure out something much more important: the format for our conversation. I briefly toyed with the idea of filming a one-off interview—"Dylan Speaks to His Troll," I'd probably title it—but I knew the video would get more views if it was part of my existing interview series. *Shutting Down Bullsh*t* came out every Friday, and each week I would sit down with progressive activists, artists, and public figures to dismantle what we considered to be socially regressive ideas. This usually meant conservative talking points. "Pronouns don't matter," I once prompted a nonbinary guest who efficiently proved that they do with a quippy comeback. "God is a straight cis white man," I said to a progressive priest who laughed at the suggestion and then proceeded to model what inclusive and affirming Christianity can look like. "All Lives Matter," I threw to an activist who laughed and then somberly explained that in a utopia that is true, but we don't live in that utopia just yet. The title of the series announced its inherent subjectivity: what my like-minded guests and I labeled "bullshit," others did not. So what prompts could I serve up to a guest like Josh who would surely disagree on what even counted as "bullshit" in the first place? Eventually I decided to go with the simplest option possible: I would break apart his message, sentence by sentence, and have him explain why he wrote it. Now, after some schedule coordination, I am thrilled to find myself here, in the studio, about to call Josh and see his face for the very first time.

After delivering my introduction, I turn to the laptop that is set up on a stool in front of me, I select his username, and I press send.

Shapes begin to pulse on the screen to indicate a call is being made, but then the shapes abruptly stop.

Call failed, the screen tells me.

"Ohhh-kay," I say jokingly in a singsong way.

Dustin laughs from behind the camera, resetting the lens. Alison smiles as she checks that the Wi-Fi is working. This isn't live so, thankfully, we can edit this out.

I press send again and the geometric shapes pulse once more. *Call failed.*

Without thinking, I impulsively click the dial button again like a toddler trying to revive a broken toy. *Call failed.*

Concerned, I open Facebook.

"Hey!" I write to Josh. "Just tried you. You ready?"

"Camera cut," Dustin announces. Alison jumps up to turn the air-conditioning back on.

His typing bubbles appear, then disappear. *Oh my God*, I think, *is he about to pull out?*

"1 sec. Fixing it," Josh finally writes back.

"Great," I say. "Let me know when you're good."

A few moments pass.

"Its being dumb," he says.

"It's okay. What can I do to help? Wanna try calling me?"

"Give me 1 sec," he types.

I give a worried smile to Alison. Dustin patiently waits by the camera to roll again.

A few minutes pass.

"Any updates?" I ask Josh.

"Wont fucking worm," he writes. "K," he sends right after, correcting his typo.

"Do you have skype set up to video on your phone?"

"Fuck!" He writes. We have unceremoniously returned to the disjointed back-and-forth of our Facebook message exchange.

"Do you have a computer you can skype on?"

"No."

"Okay," I write, and then, disappointed, I type out our last resort: "How about let's just do audio?"

I wonder for a moment if I should just cancel this shoot altogether. Without the opportunity to see Josh's face, for the audience to see us seeing each other, I don't really know the point of continuing. We've already spoken on the phone, so how could an audio-only chat be worthwhile? Plus, all of my interviews to this point have been face-to-face and while I had been comfortable with the concession of a video call—the only real option for someone who lived nearly two thousand miles away—now it seems that even that isn't possible. Mostly, I dread the silence that will haunt our conversation, the pockets of dead air that will throw me off my game. And then, just as I am about to cancel, I think of the Quakers.

◎

Quakerism was—and is—a sadly fading religion in the United States, not that it was ever hip per se, but it was far more popular in the eighteenth century than it is today. Or, for that matter, in the year 2000, when I began as a new student at a Quaker school. (This drew the expected jokes about oats.) During orientation I was introduced to the central Quaker practice of silent meeting, or as it is known more officially, Meeting for Worship. The name helpfully tells you exactly what it is: a ritual where the community comes together to sit in silence.

As preteens we would all groan when it was time for silent meeting, rolling our eyes at the injustice of making us sit still for twenty minutes at a time. Could there be anything worse? We were hormone-addled kids squirming in our rapidly changing bodies, forced to make those bodies squirm a little less. It was torture. But as I got older, I slowly came to appreciate the sanctity of this time—the rare gift of being able to sit in a room with hundreds of other members of my community intentionally doing nothing, all in silence.

But it wasn't just silence. Any participant could enter this silence by standing up to speak whatever was on their mind. An offering into the void. More religious versions of this practice explain that participants should speak when God inspires them to speak, while our secular instruction was to speak simply if we were moved to speak. Beautifully, this practice made space for both interpretations.

These offerings could be about anything that came to mind. One person might stand up to recount a mundane occurrence on their morning commute, the next might open up about a particularly painful experience they had been secretly enduring for years and were finally ready to share out loud, and a third person might stand up to articulate a revelation that was dawning on them in real time. Any discomfort that the silence may have brought faded whenever someone stood up to enter it. These offerings were invariably beautiful. Shining diamonds of revelation that lay just beyond the threshold of a moment of emptiness, the prize for enduring momentary unease. When it worked it was as if we were in a cosmic domino effect, where one thought from one person would inspire a seemingly unrelated thought in another. These offerings created a constellation of ideas, experiences, and stories—individual stars that came together to form a galaxy. And in those moments in the Quaker meetinghouse, when the stillness overtook us, when the silence was entered, when we listened to someone's words without seeing who was speaking, it was as if we were all quietly moving to music that wasn't playing but somehow we all could hear.

◎

Think of this as silent meeting, I coach myself as I plug Josh's phone number into Skype's dial pad. I press the call button and wait.

The phone rings.

"Hello?" Josh answers. *Hallelujah.*

This is my first time hearing his voice since our initial phone call two months earlier. My disappointment that I won't get to see his face for this interview fades as I now have chosen to think of him as a person entering the silence just a few rows behind me in the Quaker meetinghouse. I may not see him, but we are still fully connected.

"Hi, Josh. How are you?"

"I'm good. How are you?"

"I'm good. So, Josh, can you remember what video it was that I had made that you wrote me that initial message?"

"I'm pretty sure it had to do with your unboxing video."

"Do you know what I was unboxing?"

"It was Police Brutality."

"Okay, great." Then, changing gears to deliver the line I say at the opening of each episode: "Josh, are you ready to shut down some bullshit?"

"I am ready," Josh says.

As planned, we go through his message sentence by sentence. And each line becomes a bar of that invisible music that would play in the meetinghouse.

Youre a moron. We march toward a retraction, an explanation, and an exploration about why he was offended by a video that criticized police.

Youre the reason this country is dividing itself. In time with the silent music, we sway from a discussion about media bias to a consideration of echo chambers.

Just stop. We rotate around this topic for a while and find a moment of levity when Josh says he thought I was "ten times more famous" than I turned out to be. "I thought you were a celebrity in Hollywood, all that, so I didn't think you were actually going to read it."

Being Gay is a sin. We spin into his understanding of scripture and homophobia.

"You just have to have respect for the other person and know that whatever they think doesn't affect your life," Josh says.

"But you are disagreeing with something that is at the very core of my being," I reply. "So, how does mutual respect play into that?"

"You're just really good with these tough questions, aren't you?" Josh's voice chimes back from the laptop.

"I'm just truly curious."

"So, I shouldn't hate on you being gay because that's your choice as a human being," Josh offers as solace.

"Do you think being gay is a choice?" I offer back.

"I do," Josh says. Though we disagree, we are still somehow keeping with the beat of the music.

Then, for one final move, I want to revisit something we spoke about on our call, hoping that Josh will feel comfortable enough to explore it here, and praying that it won't mess up our tempo.

"Final question," I say. "Have you ever been bullied before like this in the form of the message you sent me?"

There is a flash of silence, a stillness. And just as I'm about to insert a caveat saying that he doesn't have to answer that if he doesn't want to, I hold myself back. And he says:

"Every day of my life."

More silence.

"Where?" I ask.

"I go to school, I come home, and I'm alone. I don't have friends to go hang out with. I've actually been called 'gay' multiple times. I've been told to drink bleach, all that fun stuff."

"So, it sucks to be treated that way, right?" I ask, setting up my next move.

"Yes, sir. And I'm guessing you're about to ask why did I do it then?" Josh has now taken the lead and he forges ahead: "I think it's just that I'm so used to it. I'm so used to getting those messages and still being able to survive through it that I'm just so angered at the world that I just take it out on you."

This conversation is unlike any other I've hosted on camera. Avatar Dylan is nowhere to be found, and without his armor I am finding it impossible to meet Josh's disagreement—even his profoundly offensive statements—with the slick venom that I would employ in a direct-to-camera monologue. This phone call makes other episodes of *Shutting Down Bullsh*t* look like relaxed Ping-Pong matches, simple back-and-forths with a ball of agreement. Here we are doing something far more complicated.

This isn't the game at all. There is nothing to be won. Success, here, is not determined by domination but by connection. Josh is no longer my opponent, but my collaborator. We are working toward the same goal, moving to the same beat. And because we are united in our desire to understand each other, we are able to momentarily step outside of our conflict in order to view it from the same vantage point. This feels like a true conversation, a throwback to Quaker meetings, which is to say it is the opposite of a game. It is a dance. And now I am ready for the final spin.

"Do you think that this will change your desire to write someone a message, a mean message, on the internet in the future?" I ask.

"Definitely," he replies. "It's going to make . . . Whenever I feel the urge to do it, I'm just going to think about everything that's happened from me doing it to you and think twice about it."

"Well, cool," I say, at a loss for a more eloquent word. "Thank you so much, and I will see you on the internet."

"See you there."

"Bye." I hang up and sit there for a moment, catching my breath.

Wordlessly, Dustin cuts the camera.

Alison looks at me to check in.

We all share a moment of silence.

Finally, Dustin enters it: "Holy shit."

◎

"Is it up?" Josh messages me two days later.

It's 2:53 P.M., more than an hour after I said our video would be posted and I understand his eager anticipation.

"Hahah. No," I type. "Export problems. Promise I'll send you the link when it's up."

I put down my phone and get back to work with Dustin who is fuming at a recurring software glitch that forces us to export our videos multiple times, adding mind-numbing hours to our already time-crunched edit schedule.

97 percent. 98 percent. 99 percent. Done.

"Finally," Dustin says, banging on the table, cursing at the editing software under his breath. "I'm gonna go have a cigarette."

As Dustin grabs his coat, the video is posted and I immediately send it to Josh.

"Wow," he writes after watching the video.

"Hope to continue the conversation," I say. "You're a great guy, Josh."

"I luv talking to you," he writes. "Hope to get more chances too."

Fortunately, I think he will. Our conversation has planted a seed in me so I walk back to my desk, open up the HATE FOLDER, and as I scroll I silently ask its members *Who else would like to dance?*

3

the everything storm

"Hi, I'm Dylan Marron and this is *Conversations with People Who Hate Me*, an interview series, where I get to know some of the people behind the most hateful and negative messages I've received on the internet."

I take a breath.

"Today, we are talking to Frank."

I am sitting in a muted gray wingback armchair beside the red Ikea nightstand that normally lives by Todd's side of the bed. On top of this nightstand sits my laptop, angled toward me and opened to Skype. Hovering just above its keyboard is a microphone that cranes to reach me with the help of its L-shaped stand. A tangle of cables runs from my laptop to the makeshift audio control center, which has been constructed on the dining room table where Todd and I typically eat home-cooked meals with our roommates, Charlotte and Yoshi, and a revolving door of friends. Todd is still up at law school taking his finals, and Charlotte and Yoshi have graciously given me the apartment for the day. Only hours earlier this looked like the cozy Brooklyn three-bedroom that we all share, the one I have lived in for five years, and in a few hours it will again. But right now it is my recording studio, and this is the first day of production on my new podcast, a social experiment that I left my job to make.

◎

About a month after my video with Josh was released I made the difficult decision to leave Seriously.TV. In some ways, it was also a decision to leave the game of the internet itself. Or, I suppose, more accurately, to create a breakout room from it. After the high of my conversation with Josh, I couldn't stop fantasizing about speaking to other members of the HATE FOLDER, the possibility of new dances with different strangers I had also written off as adversaries. What emerged was a concept for a podcast that would feature me having an in-depth conversation with a different HATE FOLDER resident in each episode. The working title for this social experiment was *Conversations with People Who Hate Me*, and day after day I combed through my options trying to figure out who might be my next dance partner.

I sifted through countless contenders. From the Australian teenager who had written, "You are the most pathetic human being I have ever seen on the internet in my entire life" to the father of two who said, "Hey faggot. You should go be the change you want to see and apply to be a police officer."

I tried to imagine the chat I might have with each of them. What might I talk about with the Midwestern grandmother? In her message to me she'd said, "YOU HAVE NOT CLUE WHAT IS GOING ON IN n[orth] d[akota] . . . STFU . . . FAGGOT" after I had made a post celebrating the temporary halt of the Dakota Access Pipeline, the proposed gas line that would cut through a sacred indigenous water source.

In my digging for potential guests, I also rediscovered some amusing gems. Like the message from a kind-looking man who had written, "Your a fucking idiot should have swallowed 9 months before your mummy gave birth to your ignorant ass." There was no punctuation in his message, but I gathered he was saying that my mother should have "swallowed" nine months before I was born, which suggests he may not know that oral sex doesn't lead to pregnancy. Perhaps on our phone call we might have a heartfelt conversation about our political differences, while also taking some time to brush up on the birds and the bees.

As I browsed their profiles, I would try to determine whether or not I felt safe inviting them to the dance floor. This was determined by three questions: One, did they have other interactions on their page? Two, did they have pictures of themselves? And three, the most dystopian consideration of all, did they seem real? But in the end, it really came down to the profoundly unscientific determinant of Gut Feeling. Once they passed this test, I would select their screenshot from the HATE FOLDER, and drag it into a PDF of potential guests for this burgeoning social experiment.

Wanting to make sure that I wasn't only speaking to people who politically disagreed with me, I also made sure to include representatives from the small but mighty caucus of the HATE FOLDER that aligned with me ideologically but opposed me on a personal level.

This subcommittee included an older gay man who had publicly posted, "For the most part, I agree with what Dylan Marron says but I want to punch out his smug, sanctimonious face whenever his videos appear on Facebook." It also featured a queer, progressive artist from Atlanta who had written, "Dylan Marron represents some of the worst aspects of liberalism." One person with a cartoon profile picture told me directly, "I hate your face, you are a horrible person to be representing LGBT people."

The simple act of building this PDF helped me reframe the contents of the HATE FOLDER as exciting opportunities, rather than the terrifying collection of digital rocks that had been hurled through my social media window. With this lens, each message began to burst with possibility.

The Midwestern grandmother's message was transformed from an alarming attack of unsolicited hostility to a fascinating entry point through which we might discuss the violent tactics employed by colonizers against indigenous populations.

The father of two who called me a "faggot" and recommended that I go join the police force might want to talk about the difference between reform and abolition.

And after browsing the profile of the older gay man who said he wanted to "punch out [my] smug, sanctimonious face," I started thinking about what a fascinating exploration we might have of the intergenerational rifts among members of the same marginalized group.

In the end, twenty-six HATE FOLDER inhabitants were granted entry to this elite PDF. And so, on a rainy spring afternoon, I began working my way through this short list to send out the first invitations to the show.

Out of the twenty people I invited that first week, a few flatly refused.

"Nope. Thanks," wrote a man who had asked me to drown myself.

"Honestly man I dont have that much of a strong enough opinion to take time out of my day to do this," replied the guy who had written an impassioned message that I was a "fuckin idiot" and "God damn PATHETIC."

The libertarian who said I was "a walking contradiction to the point that it's comical" was on board at first, calling the idea of talking to each other "refreshing and honestly exciting." Then, three days later he surprised me with another message: "I'm not comfortable doing this any longer def feels like a setup." I tried to respond, but I couldn't even type a message. He had blocked me.

Others said they would think about it and promised to get back to me later but never did, and a handful ignored my message entirely.

Still, eleven people said yes, and before I knew it, the first day of recording was upon us.

An entire crew came over to assemble the studio. Christy, the show's executive producer, showed up with light stands and coffee. Vincent, the audio engineer, unpacked a trove of fancy recording equipment from his minivan. Alen, the production manager, showed up early to make sure everything went smoothly. And Alison, our production assistant, came prepared to make all of our jobs easier. With four scheduled phone calls, there was much to be done. And with this unbeatable team, furniture was rearranged, cables were plugged in, and mic levels were tested. Cameras were also set up as the plan was to film these early calls in order to capture the glory of this new project. This, we all thought, was going to be an incredible day. Then, it began.

Recording files of the first call were accidentally wiped from a hard drive during a media transfer.

The second call never happened because my planned guest—a man who told me to "get a grip bitch" and that I was "so gross, and leaking with negativity"—completely ghosted fifteen minutes before we had agreed to speak.

With these unforeseen catastrophes, there was a lot riding on my third guest, a man named Frank who had immediately accepted my invitation when I first reached out. And now here I find myself, seconds away from dialing his number, hoping and praying that this will actually work.

◎

I look into the camera and address my future audience.

"Today we are talking to Frank. And a few weeks ago, Frank sent me this message."

I proceed to pull out the large pink index card upon which I've transcribed his qualifying remarks, a multiparagraph Facebook message that he seems to have written in a fit of rage. I read it aloud.

"'When the police aren't there sensitive young men like you will be the first to go. I have to assume you've never checked your comments or like/dislike ratio because I've never seen one so poor. I worry that you will blame this on white CIS men but please look closer. It's the people that you are championing that hate you. i.e. You are doing something very bad. Proceed.'"

I take a breath before I dive in to the second part of Frank's message.

"'Guy I'm sorry one last message you were talking with those Muslim women and you told them that there's been lots of talk about a Muslim registry and that there was a Muslim registry with George Bush. So you said a total lie that could've made them scared and made you look like a social justice warrior and American men as monsters so that's why you're a piece of shit. Good thing nobody watches your shit your so dumb you regularly say things that 100% makes the situation worse and you do it to signal how virtuous you are! Again good thing nobody watches your shit but hey you're probably getting 10 bucks a video so whatever.'"

I don't have a plan for our conversation, per se. And why would I need one? In his message alone, Frank has hit on so many topics that I'm confident we won't run out of things to talk about. Plus, after the day's earlier failures, talking to anyone about anything at all will count as a success to me.

Unlike Josh, Frank and I haven't spoken to each other at all so I have no sense of how this will go. I don't even know what he sounds like.

"Okay," I say, turning my attention from the transcribed Facebook message and back toward the camera. "We are going to call Frank right now."

I punch in the number Frank gave me, press send, and wait.

Ring.

"Hello?" a man answers, his voice thick with a distinctive accent. With just one spoken word he already reminds me of a beloved substitute teacher I had in high school, and I breathe a sigh of relief.

"Hi, is this Frank?"

"This is Frank!"

"Hi, Frank, this is Dylan Marron!" I say, figuring I should reintroduce myself. "How are you?"

"I'm doing fine, thank you!" A dog barks in the background. "Busy day. I had to fix my car and I had to fix my washing machine."

"Oh!" I yelp, delighted at this peek into the mundanity of Frank's life.

"Let me get my dogs out of the room," he says. Then, adopting a different voice, he orders "Cinnamon! Both a' yous! Go!"

I can't help but smile. A stranger with whom I seem to share nothing but an algorithmic run-in, a man who called me a "piece of shit," has a dog named Cinnamon.

This is gonna be amazing, I think to myself.

After I read Frank's message back, his laugh cracks through the phone line.

"I had a couple cocktails in me. But let me tell you, I stand by most of what I said," he confesses, still coming down from his laugh. "Not about you personally, but about"—he pauses—"Social Justice Warriors."

A *Social Justice Warrior,* or "SJW" as the term is often abbreviated in online parlance, is a person who fights against social injustice. It sounds like a noble title, but the term is meant as a put-down. Popular YouTube compilations document "SJW Cringe Moments," and these supercuts feature clips of progressive people having strong emotional reactions on camera—whether they are taking part in protests, vehemently advocating for equality in a vlog, or simply speaking in a way that the video maker has deemed "cringeworthy." The term has been leveled against me in the past, but I've never minded it. What better cause could one serve?

I am ready to jump in and challenge Frank on his view of Social Justice Warriors, but just as I'm about to reply, I remind myself to simply let him talk. This, I am sure, will allow us to find our rhythm. So, I opt to begin a mental list of topics I'd like to engage him on later.

SJWism, my brain jots down.

Frank continues to elaborate on his distaste for Social Justice Warriors. "Certain people want to turn over the whole country in order to solve small problems. Let me give you an example: the LGBT community. L-G-B-T . . . whatever letters they're adding onto it now."

Oh, dear. It's the dreaded there-are-too-many-letters joke. This is a familiar one for any breathing queer person who has ever attended a family dinner, been on social media, or met another human being.

Too many letters, my mind adds to the list of future talking points. I let him continue.

"There's always been gay people, they've been getting along fine in life. And I'm a supporter of gay marriage by the way, but I don't think that they need a whole list of rights. They're *people*. It's like saying 'redhead rights,' or 'left-handed people rights.' It just seems all silly to me. The whole social justice stuff seems silly to me."

What does he mean about queer people "getting along fine in life?" Is he aware of how many LGBT kids make up homeless youth after they've been kicked out of their homes? Does he know that, right now at this very moment, in 2017, it's legal to be fired in some states simply for being gay? Can he fathom the risk of violence that trans people face? I wish I had a handy statistic about any of these topics that I could whip out right now. As I wait for my brain to remember one, I figure that I might as well add them to the list.

Getting along fine and *homelessness* and *gay jobs* and *gay fire* and *transphobia*, my brain jots down.

"I'm against things like Black Lives Matter," Frank declares as he wraps up his thoughts on social justice.

My stomach tightens. The popular Desmond Tutu quote "If you are neutral in situations of injustice, you have chosen the side of the oppressor" pops in my head. What would my future audience say if I stay silent? So, resolving to not align myself with the oppressor, I push back.

"Saying that 'Black Lives Matter is a problem' is tough to hear only because I feel like that is a movement that is rooted in just saying a group of people's lives matter. And you disagree with that?" I ask, hoping he'll say no.

"No, of course I don't disagree with that," he says. *Phew.* "But I'm saying that what they concentrate on is the minutiae of the killings."

Minutiae of the killings?! My brain screams. I want to list the names of unarmed Black people killed by police and ask him: "Is this 'minutiae' to you?!" I want to immediately serve him with a devastating fact about the disproportionate state violence that Black people face every day. I do my best to recall any statistics from Michelle Alexander's *The New Jim Crow* but can't. Then, in the absence of hard data, I try to quickly come up with a retort that meets his statement with the comeback it deserves, but again my mind is blank. I am growing homesick for my old stomping ground of a video script or a tweet—mediums that grant me the ability to research, sharpen, and polish my responses before I publish them. Unfortunately, this conversation is happening in real time, so all I can do is let the moment pass me by.

"Have you ever been called racist?" I ask, adding *minutiae* to the list in the hopes that a statistic or cutting barb will magically reveal itself to me later.

"Sure. All the time online." He says this matter-of-factly. "But I don't think of myself as a racist."

"But you feel—"

"I think most people aren't really racist. I mean everyone has a little bit, but . . ." Frank trails off.

I add *inherent racism* and *white supremacy* to the list.

"I think that a lot of the racists are strawmen. When they say 'oh K-K-K, Fascist U-S-A,' well, who's the KKK? Thirty guys down south with pickup trucks? They're strawmen. They don't really exist."

"I mean, I think, sadly, it's more than thirty guys," I say, trying to conjure up that map from the Southern Poverty Law Center, the one that shows how many active white supremacist groups exist in the United States.

"Well. Maybe," he semi-concedes.

We then skim a host of other issues, never really engaging with them past their headline.

"I have more a problem with illegal aliens!" Frank jokes, while making the case that he wasn't trying to vilify Black people because "they're Americans."

Xenophobia, I add to my list.

"If we make everybody an American, then being an American is going to lose its value," he says matter-of-factly after softening his stance on undocumented immigrants.

Patriotism by exclusion, my brain scribbles quickly.

"Now they're all rich! Now they're all casino owners!" he quips about Native Americans.

Colonialism and *poverty among native populations.*

"I'm a fan of fossil fuels," he says, in response to me asking how he feels about the Dakota Access Pipeline.

I've truly never heard anyone say this out loud. So, I add *fracking* to the list, trying to recall what the term actually means.

A quick glance at the time tells me that we are thirty-three minutes into our conversation, halfway through our allotted time.

Hoping to focus on one of the previous topics we touched on, I begin to review the list I've been gathering in my head, only to discover there are many more topics than I had anticipated. Where do I even begin? Should I start with *white supremacy* or *homelessness of queer youth*? Or should I work backward and discuss *colonialism* and then the *hierarchy of immigrants*? I don't know how to choose. Each topic is just as vital as the one before it.

"If you are neutral in situations of injustice, you have chosen the side of the oppressor," Desmond Tutu's voice booms to me, reverberating through the halls of history. I can picture him shaking his head, disapprovingly.

I try to devise some magical question that singlehandedly allows us to cover queer homelessness *and* Black Lives Matter *and* fracking. What only moments earlier was a promising list of topics to revisit, is now a cyclone of talking points, hovering just above us. Now, each potential avenue of conversation looks more like a violent airstream than a promising path forward. And just as a tornado can turn an otherwise harmless object into a lethal projectile, the gusty winds of our chaotic conversation threaten to transform an otherwise harmless follow-up question into a never-ending rabbit hole.

Where do I even begin?

There is a rising tension between everything we *should* discuss and what we actually have *time* to discuss, and this tension transforms our would-be topics into moisture. And just like that, it begins to pour with a bounty of current events and social ills so overwhelming that I don't know what to do. Then, I look up and see it: the dark gray cloud of everything we could and should talk about, all of the topics that social media tells me "demand my attention," every half-remembered statistic, that funny Twitter retort that once made me laugh, every article I skimmed, every joke I've seen on late night television, and every infographic that I can vaguely recall.

I know what this is. It's there every time I wake up on a free day and somehow end up doing nothing at all. I have gotten caught in it when I sit down to watch something on Netflix, and, after scrolling through the endless options for thirty minutes, settle on the same classic movie I've already seen countless times. I am powerless to its gravitational pull whenever I face a blank Word document whose white void renders me incapable of writing anything at all.

This is the Everything Storm. And I have led us right into its eye.

Through the thick sheets of cascading potential topics, I can't actually see Frank. I can only make out the vague shape of someone who disagrees with me. I know he thinks that the KKK doesn't really exist anymore, but *why*? I know he doesn't understand LGBTQIA+ rights beyond marriage, but where does his confusion come from? *Why* is he a fan of fossil fuels? Who is he? What drives him? Just as the Everything Storm can stalk a brand-new day bursting with potential, movie selection, and a blank Word document, I'm seeing that it can rip into conversation, too.

Now I need to get us out of it.

"So, Frank," I say, trying to fit us under an umbrella. "It feels like there's a lot that we, like, so strongly disagree about. Right?"

"I know."

"How do you think someone like you and someone like me can keep having productive conversations?"

"Well," he says, after a contemplative pause, "I think we're having a decent conversation now." His answer is earnest and sincere.

"Yeah," I say, grateful that he thinks so.

"By being civil," Frank elaborates. "By not saying things like I said to you when I texted you." A laugh breaks apart his sentence. In his voice I hear a refreshing self-awareness and an acknowledgment of how wild it is that we're actually speaking to each other.

He's not wrong. We aren't yelling at each other, nor are we calling each other names. But I don't know that civility is the cure-all for the Storm. To me, civility is more like a pleasant temperature—a lovely component to good weather, but not good weather itself. After all, a hurricane in 72 degrees is still a hurricane.

"I actually agree with you about being civil," I begin. "But I also just want to say, I think the viewpoints that I have don't have a direct impact on your life, right? Like, they don't—my viewpoints don't change your way of life, right?"

"Not at all. No, sir."

Focus, Dylan.

"So, let's take one specific thing you brought up," I begin. "Saying that the LGBTQIA-plus community—"

Frank laughs.

"Yes!" I exclaim firmly, hoping to prevent a revival of the alphabet soup joke. "Those are the letters in the acronym!"

"What are they again? Give it to me one more time so I get them right?"

"Oh wow!" I exclaim, surprised by what seems to be genuine interest. "Okay great. L-G—" I get flustered and start over. "L-G-B-T— Oh my God, *I'm* getting it wrong now!"

"It's not easy!" Frank jokes back.

I gather myself and start again. "L-G-B-T-Q-I-A-plus," I say slowly and carefully, sensing the entire queer community depending on me to get it right this time.

"Q . . . I . . . A . . . plus," Frank repeats back deliberately, as if he's confirming a phone number I've just given him. It sounds like he's truly writing this down. "So, what is the 'I,' and the 'A,' and the 'plus'?"

"Great questions," I affirm, shocked but delighted. "'I' is *intersex*. The 'A' is *asexual*. And the 'plus' is kind of getting ahead of ourselves— knowing that there are other people involved in this acronym that we might not be identifying yet."

"Got you. See, it used to be," Frank begins, "'Heterosexual Male,' 'Heterosexual Female,' 'Homosexual Male,' 'Homosexual Female.' So, I'll catch up. I have no problem with that."

Sexuality and gender are different things, I jot down on my mental list, which immediately triggers an unmistakable growl of thunder in the distance, and I quickly erase it.

Since we seem to be moving along well by focusing on this one topic, I decide to revisit something he mentioned earlier.

"You said 'These are of course important issues, but we don't need to talk about them.' What do you mean by that?"

"I mean, like I was saying before—gay rights—it's almost like left-handed rights and right-handed rights and redhead rights. It's something that we don't always have to . . ." He trails off. "What rights are you talking about? I understand the right to marry. And, okay, there's a bathroom issue. I understand there's a bathroom issue. But you see these people and they're fighting for these rights but they have the rights already. What rights are we talking about? I don't understand what rights they're talking about. What rights do gays need that they don't have now?"

My brain is pinging with Everythings to discuss. Talking points flood my synapses, along with every zinger, clever meme, and shiny infographic I can think to call upon. They are loud and persistent.

Just respond to his question, I tell myself.

"Well, I can tell you, if you're—"

"Tell me!" he pleads, curiosity undergirding his excitement.

"Just because I have the right to marry doesn't necessarily mean that legislation is leading the way in protecting me if I am the victim of a hate crime," I say, trying to be as measured and calm as possible. "I think it *is* important to, in fact, talk about these issues because there are issues that affect people based on their identity. Do you disagree?"

"Yes, but yes and no. And I'll tell you why: because *crimes* exist," he says. "And as far as gay men being able to hold hands in society, the government can't dictate how that happens. Society has to change. And it is changing."

"You are not a gay man, right?" I ask, even though I know the answer from browsing his profile.

"No. I am a cisgendered straight male, married for twenty years to a beautiful liberal tree-hugging wife who I love."

I don't know what shocks me more, the fact that he has a liberal wife or that he has now used variations of the word "cisgender" twice— first in his initial message to me and now again as he described himself.

Focus, Dylan.

"The only reason I asked that is to say that I *am* a gay man, and I understand that laws protect against crime, but my husband and I don't hold hands in the street because of the shit we get for it."

"And your opinion has much more validity than mine does in this area. I have no problem bowing to your experience in this area."

Is that a crack of sunlight? Do I hear a bird chirping in the distance? I had been so invested in steadying our umbrella, that only now can I see that the Storm has passed. Without its roar I can more clearly hear him—his cadence, his tone, his resignation, his excitement. And since we no longer run the risk of slipping, we are finally dancing.

With the opportunity afforded by this newfound sunshine, I decide to revive a topic from earlier. "Would you be willing to apply the same generosity that you just gave to me by saying that my opinion is more valid in this area when you're talking about things like Black Lives Matter to a Black person who is—"

"I *would*," Frank says, cutting me off, "except that a lot of people, definitely a good percentage of Black people, do not support Black Lives Matter. A good portion of Black people voted for Donald Trump. Maybe not all of them. Maybe not half of them, but I don't feel that Black Lives Matter has the eyes and ears of the entire Black community. I don't feel that way at all."

A few droplets land on my face and I guiltily accept that I won't be able to change his mind about this in the course of our phone call.

"When did you start identifying as a conservative?" I ask, in an attempt to ground us in personal experience.

"It happened later in life and I'll tell ya: I was a liberal, I was pro-choice. I was very, very liberal and outspoken about it until I was about thirty-five years old," Frank says. "I used to be very pro-choice, and I would look in the science books for children, gestation, and when it begins, and when the heartbeat begins, and when brain waves begin, and it just occurred to me that life begins at conception. Life begins at conception."

My brain is now pinging with questions that I want to ask him, but unlike the unfocused Everythings, these new questions come from a genuine desire to know him. Who was that thirty-five-year-old Frank? What did his ideological support system look like then and what does it look like now? How did this one realization lead to adopting an entire conservative identity? How does the Frank of today regard the Frank of yesterday? What is his media diet? Unfortunately, though, we're at the end of our call and all of these potential avenues serve as bittersweet reminders of the conversation we could have had if the Everything Storm hadn't derailed us.

"Has this conversation helped you at all?" I ask out of true curiosity.

"I think so. I think so. Just to show that two people—so ideologically polarized—can have a good conversation without shouting 'racist,' 'dirtbag,' to each other. I think there's something good there. There's something good there." His second repetition is soft and contemplative.

"So, Frank," I say, changing gears, "this podcast is actually called *Conversations with People Who Hate Me*. Do you hate me?"

Frank breaks out into a big clap of laughter.

"Do you hate me?" I press.

"In order to put it on, do I have to say 'yes'? 'Cause I will!"

"No, in fact. I—no, no! Don't—" I try to explain.

"I no longer hate you, Dylan!"

"You 'no longer' hate me! So you *did* . . . ?"

"You won! You won!"

"No, wait, no no!" I plead. "It's not about winning or losing! It's—"

"You know why? Because you're willing to listen. I'm listening to you, you're listening to me, and that's the most important thing."

I look at the time and know that I should begin preparing for my next guest. So, we say our goodbyes and conclude our dance, however rain-soaked it may have been.

"Keep up the bad work!" Frank says as he signs off, a throwback to what he had written to me in his initial message.

I hang up our call and stretch my arms, looking out to the assembled crew, exhausted yet invigorated. Still damp from the Storm, but triumphant for having weathered it.

◉

The next day, eager to listen to our conversation with fresh ears, I station myself at my desk, plug in my headphones, and begin the editing process. If during our call I was a field researcher caught in a Storm, I am now a weather correspondent reporting on location the following morning, picking up the pieces and assessing the damage.

I review the whole interview and once I'm finished, I immediately yank the headphones out of my ears and lean back in my chair with a frustrated sigh. The Everything Storm's distinct rumble is present throughout our conversation, and I don't know how I can salvage it.

I have two options: immediately quit this project and go live in a cave for the rest of eternity, or take a twenty-minute break. Fantasizing about the former, I opt for the latter and grab my phone before dramatically collapsing on the couch.

As I lie down, my slack face illuminated by the fluorescent glow of my phone, I scroll past a video of Sally Yates's testimony, articles about the flurry of conservative judges that Trump will likely appoint, and a trending hashtag #4WordLetDowns. "There's no more food," the *BuzzFeed* account shares along with a GIF of SpongeBob SquarePants sitting alone at a restaurant. I scroll past a social media celebrity re-creating the upside-down Spider-Man kiss with her husband, a *New York Times* tweet about the three hundred young Nigerian schoolgirls kidnapped by Boko Haram, and then I see that John Oliver is trending. I click on his name, which takes me to a link that opens the YouTube app on my phone.

I let Oliver explain net neutrality to me but I stop in the middle of his monologue to search for a video he references—Taylor Swift's 2012 song "I Knew You Were Trouble" reedited to feature a goat's bleat instead of the chorus. Once I'm done, I return to Oliver's explainer. Upon completion, the side panel prompts me to watch more videos of his. And I do. I watch his exposé of Jared Kushner and Ivanka Trump, followed by an explainer of how the French presidential elections could determine the fate of the European Union. I watch Stephen Colbert joke about Cinco de Mayo, Samantha Bee celebrate journalism, and Trevor Noah discuss North Korea. I watch Jimmy Fallon play a game called "slapjack" with Chris Pine, which, as Fallon explains, "Works the same as blackjack, but at the end of each round the winner gets to slap the loser across the face with a giant prosthetic hand." I watch Jimmy Kimmel deliver an impassioned monologue about healthcare.

Then, somewhere between intending to Google "what is a deductible" and actually doing it, I have that stomach-dropping sensation that one gets at the end of a horror movie when the protagonist and their sidekick have finally escaped the villain only to discover that the sidekick was actually the villain all along. I am staring directly at the genesis of the Everything Storm.

If our primary job as citizens of the public square is to keep up, then the Everything Storm is produced by the tension between the pressure to do so and the illusion that it's possible.

In the age of the internet, though, the very notion of "keeping up" is unrealistic. Social media is a multibillion-member brain trust that encourages each member to constantly contribute thoughts, jokes, and opinions as soon as they are conceived. Trying to stay abreast of social media is like attempting to keep up with a squadron of Olympians all sprinting at record-breaking speeds in different directions. Unfortunately, we are fed the myth that "everyone" is keeping up with the Everythings because we have a poor sense of scale online—a topic discussed by a handful of people ends up being monolithically described as "what everyone is talking about" so we rush to join in. But no one is truly keeping up with *everything* on their own, not even the late-night hosts, who are sold to us as the effortlessly hilarious, ferociously smart "everyman," who happens to casually be a one-person human encyclopedia. This illusion is only possible because of an unseen army of researchers, writers, and producers. Each setup of a joke is vetted by one team, each punch line is carefully crafted by another, and the third makes sure it all goes smoothly.

But if the illusion of staying on the ball propels the Everything Storm, it doesn't do so alone. Another key contributor to its velocity is the noble desire to speak up. Thinking back to my conversation with Frank, I recall the moments when I wished I had a statistic, joke, or retort at the ready, but didn't. How disappointed I was in myself, and how disappointed I had surely made my future audience.

"If you are neutral in situations of injustice, you have chosen the side of the oppressor," the hologram of Desmond Tutu whispered to me during my phone call with Frank. This quote has been repurposed to condemn us for not clapping back fast enough, not biting back hard enough, not speaking when we should. But while the underlying sentiment is appropriate in context—South African apartheid—it becomes harder to apply it to every instance of injustice on the internet. In the age of social media, what counts as silence? Is silence not posting all the time? Not biting back at every disagreeable phrase uttered in a one-on-one conversation?

Perhaps I had been so taken by the poetry of this phrase that I applied it too literally, misguidedly believing that it meant I should shout as loudly as possible about every injustice I encounter, thinking that doing so is the purest form of activism.

To judge ourselves against the pace of late night hosts, millions of social media users, and poetic mandates from history is to create a recipe for burnout. This is the strange conundrum of living in the age of information: Technically, yes, we have all of the information at our fingertips. Practically speaking, though, we cannot possibly consume it all, much less understand it well enough to compellingly argue our case in a conversation about *everything*.

The *choice overload* hypothesis is the psychological concept that tells us that while having more options may seem better, it can actually be worse when it comes to decision-making. A 2000 study from psychologists Sheena Iyengar and Mark Lepper put this hypothesis to the test with food shoppers, students, and chocolate enthusiasts. At the grocery store Iyengar and Lepper found that while a display of twenty-four jams enticed more customers to stop by than the display of six jams, only 3 percent ended up buying jams when there were more options, whereas nearly 30 percent made a purchase when there were fewer. More students turned in an extra credit essay when there were fewer topics to choose from, and in the chocolate study, participants with fewer options reported higher satisfaction than those with more. More things to choose from, Iyengar and Lepper conclude, "may sometimes have detrimental consequences for human motivation."

The psychology professor Barry Schwartz has given this a helpful name: the Paradox of Choice. "With so many options to choose from, people find it very difficult to choose at all," Schwartz said in his 2005 TED Talk.

To venture into conversation, especially with our political opposites, is to face the paradox of choice at every turn. When faced with the possibility of talking about *anything*, we will invariably take it as a cue to talk about *everything*, which, as I am now learning, incurs the Storm, condemning us to talk about nothing.

This ideological weather formation isn't new. Everything has been happening all the time for as long as time has been recorded and as long as things have been occurring. Still, the Storm has undeniably gotten more relentless now that we communicate on digital platforms that both report on the Everythings as soon as they occur and subsequently entice us to express our takes on those Everythings as soon as we possibly can. Our devices have become both the Doppler radars that track the Storm and the accelerants of the Storm themselves.

So, what's the solution? Do I need to become a one-person Wikipedia? Should I find a way to insert a microchip of the entire internet into my head? Should I hire a team of fifty researchers, writers, and producers who will sit in on each of my calls?

Perhaps the solution is not to outrun the Storm or avoid it but to find out how to exist within it. The Storm will always be there, wailing outside the walls of our brain. Maybe there's no such thing as an escape. As I learned with Frank, we cannot tackle everything at once, no matter how vital or pressing those Everythings may be. So, in a climate where the Everything Storm is inevitable, the only solution is to focus, to listen, and to let it pass.

I muster up the energy to return to my desk and re-listen to the end of our conversation.

"So, Frank, this podcast is actually called *Conversations with People Who Hate Me*. Do you hate me?"

I hear his laugh again, now recorded and dancing through my headphones.

"I no longer hate you... You won! You won!"

". . . it's not about winning or losing! It's—"

"You know why? Because you're willing to listen. I'm listening to you, you're listening to me, and that's the most important thing."

4

the seeds of hate

"What?! No! I don't hate you."

Today is the podcast's third day of production and I'm on the phone with my second guest of the day, a college student named Adam. I've just revealed to him that the podcast he's on is called *Conversations with People Who Hate Me*. Adam is not taking this news like I thought he would.

Since speaking to Frank, I've recorded a number of other conversations with HATE FOLDER members. I spoke to Anna, a teacher who had found me snarky and off-putting. Josh and I recorded another phone call, where we were able to dive deeper into our explorations of religion, bullying, and political division. And, just before this call with Adam, I had spoken to Matthew, a queer liberal artist, who had publicly posted "Dylan Marron represents some of the worst aspects of liberalism." So far the title's revelation has been met with varying levels of amusement. Frank laughed. Matthew chuckled. Anna gasped in shock and said, "No! I don't hate you!" and then, without missing a beat, followed up with "I don't even hate my ex-boyfriend. I just feel sorry for him 'cause he's missing out on all this."

I had intentionally withheld the podcast's name from my guests partly because there was a chance it was temporary, but mostly because I wanted to reveal it in the eleventh hour as a springboard to the project's big question: "Do you hate me?"

Now, though, as I sit here waiting for Adam's laugh, I hear nothing. Not even a faint chuckle. There is no quick retort. All I hear is silence.

I quickly glance at the Facebook message that qualified him to be on the show in the first place, now wondering if I had completely misinterpreted it. "Being gay is a chemicals thing in your body, but similar to addictions that people have, it's an addiction you can control," I read from the piece of paper that lays on the table before me, transcribed from the message Adam had written to me weeks earlier.

It doesn't seem like there is any misinterpretation. After all, likening sexuality to a curable addiction is the underlying mentality that fuels arguments for conversion therapy, the abusive practice that falsely claims to change the sexual orientation of its participants. But to be fair, Adam isn't actively advocating for conversion therapy. Plus, in the next line of his message he had written, "I am a Christian, and I do believe homosexuality is a sin, but I also know and want you to know that God loves you."

This confusing dichotomy has been present throughout our conversation today. Earlier in our call Adam had said, "I don't agree with part of your lifestyle, but I still love you as a person." So, what is this? Is it love or hate?

I root myself back in the present moment, searching for a way to explain to Adam why I read his message as hateful.

"You are such a good human, right? I hear that on this call," I begin, hoping that a genuine affirmation might help the medicine go down. But I suppose I'm also buying time as I figure out how to encourage him to see the harm of his message without villainizing him and pushing him away. *Think, think, think,* I tell the neurons in my brain. "I think what makes me a little nervous about your message to me is that even though this sentiment from the Bible has manifested [in] you in a way that *you* say is loving, I feel like this is also sometimes the same seed that can sprout into hate."

I continue: "Thinking that homosexuality, queerness, is an urge that people can control—I believe that that is a seed that can sprout into a hatred of other people," I explain, slowly building this idea as I go. "Even though you're saying 'I love you, even though you're sinning by being gay,' that doesn't sit well fully, right? There's a bitter taste at the end of that. It's like, well, then you don't fully love me because this is part of who I am. Do you know what I mean?"

"I see where you're coming from." Adam says this slowly and distantly, like he's absorbing this new idea in real time. "That makes a lot more sense. Okay."

I recognize this must be a lot for him to take in. Adam is being asked to reconsider something that he has likely been sold as undeniable truth all his life. I don't want to overwhelm or berate him. Instead, I want to actually get through to him.

"I'm not just putting this on you," I begin. "You are not the one who came up with this idea." These phone calls have been teaching me the value of distinguishing between the system and the individual, the big and the small, the person and the hate. Or, I suppose, *alleged* hate.

Adam did not invent homophobia. It is clear he is simply repeating to me ideas he learned from the leaders of his community, who themselves were repeating what *they* had been taught. By creating a distance between Adam and homophobia, I'm inviting us to step outside of our disagreement and see it together from a more subjective lens—as if we're fellow museumgoers gazing at some big steel structure in the middle of a gallery, whispering observations to each other about its contours.

I try a more personal appeal: "I worry about the young people in communities like yours who are getting messages like these said to them by people far less loving than you, right? And I worry that that makes them feel like total outcasts. It makes them feel like there's something inherently wrong with who they are."

Seconds of silence drag on for a short eternity.

Finally, Adam responds, "That does make sense, and I hear now where you're coming from." I'm not fully convinced, but he continues: "Yeah, it's not fair. It really isn't. But that is what I believe." He says this as if it is an unalterable fact about him. As if he was born with this seed and harvesting it is his destiny. As if this belief, this thing he has been taught, is an objective truth. The sun rises, we breathe air, and being gay is a curable affliction.

I wonder for a moment if he's thinking the same thing about me, that I am speaking about my sexuality as if it is this unchangeable part of who I am when he believes it to be the exact opposite.

"But yes," he continues, "I completely understand that I am excluding and disagreeing with a crucial part of who you are. And I realize that does hurt and I in no way intended for that to become something that is hatred."

This is no small thing for Adam to say and I appreciate that he is even attempting to engage with an idea that goes against so much of what he has understood to be true.

"Well, I don't think it's manifesting as hatred in you, right? Because I think at your true core, you are a loving person. But I also worry about how that seed expresses itself in someone who isn't as loving as you, right?"

"Yeah." Adam sighs.

"I think there are some people in your community who are looking to hate people and that seed can sprout as hate in them."

"I gotcha," Adam says. "And the people that I think you're talking about is very similar to the people who have become the West Bas—or the West Baptist Church, I think, or . . ." he trails off.

"You mean the Westboro Baptist Church?" I ask, assuming he's alluding to the infamous group known for their tricolored signs that proudly proclaim "God Hates Fags" in aggressively large block lettering.

"Yes, yes. That one," Adam says.

"I think that's a great way to identify it. That same seed that you are kind of carrying," I say, "they're carrying that seed differently."

"Yeah," Adam says. He sounds sad and disappointed.

As our conversation continues to wind down, I sense him trying to get off the phone. His answers are shorter, the gaps of silence after my questions are longer, and he sounds much less animated than he had been earlier in our call. A wave of guilt comes over me. *Was I too hard on him?*

"Is there anything that you're going to do differently after this conversation?" I ask.

"Um," he begins and then laughs as if the question is so big that he doesn't even know how to begin answering it. "I'm really not sure. I know I'm still going to love people. I'll have a conversation with my pastor and just talk about what are different ways about going about this."

I suppose that's all I can ask for. And with that we say our goodbyes and hang up.

"Hey Adam. That was a challenging but I think very important conversation to have," I message him shortly after the call ends.

"Hard, but good!" He writes back. "I only would caution the title hate. What about 'Difficult Conversations'? But again, it's not my podcast! Thanks for having that conversation!"

After spending significant energy on the call justifying to Adam why I chose the word "hate" for the title, now I think I need to do the harder work of justifying it to myself.

◎

A few days have passed since our call and I find myself sitting at my desk unable to start my work. I can't get Adam's shock out of my head. *Is he right? Is the title unfair to my guests?* I entertain his alternative suggestion of *Difficult Conversations* but all I can picture is a public radio show hosted by a self-identified "empath" who meaningfully touches their chest, squints their eyes, and vigorously nods as their guests speak. Perhaps that is the type of show I'll make in the future— once I've graduated to exclusively drinking out of mugs unironically adorned with inspirational phrases—but it's not *this* show.

It occurs to me that I don't actually know the official definition of this simple word that has sparked so many questions.

"Hate," I hastily type into Google's search bar.

"Intense or passionate dislike," Google replies.

"Hatred or hate is a deep and extreme emotional dislike. It can be directed against individuals, groups, entities, objects, behaviors, or ideas. Hatred is often associated with feelings of anger, disgust, and a disposition towards hostility," Wikipedia chimes in through a sidebar.

I click on the News tab to see how this word is being used in current events.

"Frequency of Noose Hate Crime Incidents Surges," the Southern Poverty Law Center reports.

"Alt-Right, White Nationalist, Free Speech: The Far Right's Language Explained," an NPR piece teases. When I click on it I see a subsection that breaks down the difference between free speech and hate speech.

"Kansas Jayhawks: Why Kansas Fans Still Hate Missouri," a recent entry from a sports blog reads about a rivalry between two college football teams.

The word seems to cover a large range: from racist hate crimes to athletic opposition.

A few inches to the right of the Google news results I see the HATE FOLDER just sitting there on my desktop. Surely, I think, I will find some clarity in this container that started it all.

I click on it, not knowing exactly what I'm looking for. Perhaps scrolling through it for the millionth time will lead me to the clarity I seek. And so, like a geologist testing a sample of dirt to understand the larger terrain, I select four random screenshots.

"Please decapitate yourself," reads a three-word note from a stranger named Ryan.

Okay, I think, *that is for sure hate.*

"You're a piece of shit," Frank's message says.

Yup. That, too.

"Sending a hitman after you," a Facebook user named Mike warns me.

The definition of hate if I've ever seen it.

"dylan marron is so annoying," a tweet from a woman named Kyla reads.

Hmm.

Like the news articles, this range is much bigger than I thought it would be. In this light, Kyla calling me "annoying" seems harmless in comparison to Frank's more direct opinion. But Frank's message doesn't hold a candle to the graphic visual of Ryan's "please decapitate yourself," which at least puts the onus on me to end my own life, unlike Mike who has apparently taken care of that task himself.

They do, however, make sense in pairs. Kyla doesn't look so out of place next to Frank and it's understandable that Frank has been sorted in a folder with Ryan. Ryan and Mike fit with each other because both wish to see me dead, however different their tactics to fulfill that wish may be. But while the distance between each of them may be incremental, the gulf between Kyla and Mike is almost unfathomable. As I look at it now, with the distance of time, I can clearly see that "dylan marron is so annoying" exists in a different moral universe from "sending a hitman after you," yet I still apparently banished both of them to the same digital penitentiary I had constructed on my desktop.

I click on a few more HATE FOLDER installments and find something even more out of place than Kyla's benign assertion that I'm annoying.

"Dylan. Stop justifying your fuckup. Take a few days. Think about it."

"Your decision was based 100% on ableist bullshit. So we're clear."

"I'm so so sad about this video."

My stomach tightens. I know exactly what these are in reference to, and I'm embarrassed to even find them here. Earlier in the year I had produced a video about autism where I unknowingly fell into a number of ableist trends that some autistic viewers found offensive. For one thing, I invited my autistic guest's not-autistic dad to come in and explain more about autism. In the edit I made it so that the father's audio played over footage of my interview with his son. I also framed the interview as if my guest was the sole spokesperson for autism, when in reality it's a disability that many people live with in many different ways. These comments that I'm now rediscovering in my HATE FOLDER are not from detractors, but fans of mine who were alerting me that I had missed the mark. This is clearly constructive criticism, born of a genuine hurt that *I* had caused *them* and still, in the moment of receiving this feedback, I must have sorted them into this container that also housed death threats and homophobic jabs. Quickly, I remove them, but it does make me wonder: *What* doesn't *count as hate?*

As a kid I would sometimes scream "I hate you!" to my parents at the top of my lungs. The trigger for this varied. Maybe they had broken the news to me that a playdate needed to be rescheduled, or maybe my television privileges had been revoked until I did my homework. I probably said it, too, when they sat me down to review our new holiday itinerary during the first year of their divorce. Of course, I didn't mean that I hated them literally. To be honest, I don't think I knew what I meant. Maybe it was the preternatural entitlement that is found in only children, but I think it was something else: "Hate" was the only shorthand I had to express such big and indescribable feelings. Because I couldn't yet say "I am feeling something so profound and complex, the scope of which my burgeoning emotional vocabulary does not contain the words to describe, but if you'll be so kind as to give me space to process these emotions, I will accurately diagnose what is happening to me," I just said, "I hate you," instead. The closest approximation.

I wonder if a similar phenomenon was happening when this constant barrage of digital negativity came my way at such a fast rate. That in its relentlessness it became impossible to distinguish the level of severity of each comment or message. Perhaps, like my gestating mind in childhood, my developing digital mind didn't know how to process such a huge volume of criticism. So, instead of calling the folder on my desktop the "WIDE SPECTRUM OF DIGITAL NEGATIVITY THAT RANGES FROM MILD GRIEVANCE TO LITERAL DEATH THREATS OH AND ALSO TOTALLY JUSTIFIED CRITICISM, ALL OF WHICH COME FROM INDIVIDUAL HUMANS WITH THEIR OWN UNIQUE BACKSTORIES AND EXPERIENCES FOLDER," I instead simply called it the HATE FOLDER, which got the job done much quicker.

In January 2016, the social psychologist Nick Haslam coined the term "concept creep" in a research paper that sought to explain the evolving definitions of abuse, bullying, trauma, mental disorder, addiction, and prejudice. "Concepts that refer to the negative aspects of human experience and behavior," Haslam writes, "have expanded their meanings so that they now encompass a much broader range of phenomena than before." By Haslam's definition, am I contributing to the creeping expansion of the word "hate"?

Colloquially the word seems to be elastic. It can describe the Ku Klux Klan or a highly anticipated movie that fell short of expectations. It seems that we as a culture have not yet settled on a common understanding of what this word actually means.

Over the next few weeks, I privately mull over the idea of changing the show's title, but before I know it weeks turn into months and the show's debut is finally here.

◉

It's the morning of July 31, 2017. The first episode has just been released hours ago and my phone chimes with an email from Christine, the show's publicist.

"Great piece here," she says before providing a link. I click it and see a high resolution production photo of me laughing during one of the recorded calls. Just above it is the article's headline: "The Man Who Calls His Trolls to Talk It Out."

"I'm SO excited for you!" Christine says after I thank her. I'm excited, too, but this excitement is mixed in with something else. What exactly, I'm not quite sure.

It's Tuesday, August 8, and *USA Today* selects the show as their weekly podcast pick. "Engaging with internet trolls is rarely a good idea," the piece begins. "But video producer Dylan Marron decided to do just that in his self-explanatory new podcast, *Conversations with People Who Hate Me.*"

I know I should be thrilled, but there it is again: that same feeling in the pit of my stomach. Excitement with an asterisk.

It's Friday, August 11, and I learn that the *Guardian* has selected the show as their pick of the week. "Foosball fanatics, talking to trolls, and a game of thrones—best podcasts of the week" the piece teases above another picture of me smiling.

That tightness is back. *What is up with me?* I wonder. It's unlike me to dislike attention. (Recall: only child.) *Did I maybe give a bad quote or say something insensitive?* I carefully reread these three articles to figure out what exactly is bothering me so much.

"The Man Who Calls His Trolls to Talk It Out," I read semi-aloud under my breath.

"Engaging with internet trolls is rarely a good idea . . ."

". . . talking to trolls."

I now see the common denominator.

I hadn't questioned the term until my first conversation with Josh. I had, after all, titled the video of the slideshow "Empathy for My Trolls" without thinking twice about it. And why would I? It was easy to call my detractors "trolls" when they were just screenshots. Two months later when it came time to title that first video with Josh, I called it "Shutting Down Bullsh*t with a Guy Who Trolled Me," demoting the word from a noun to a verb. But as I began to mount the podcast, and as I was speaking with the so-called "trolls" in question, I started to feel differently. Now seeing the word used in the press makes me want to remove the word from my lexicon altogether.

Partly, this is for practical production reasons. This show won't exist without my guests and nobody will want to be part of this if I say, "Hey! I'm making a podcast where I talk to trolls. I would love to speak with you!" That would be akin to inviting someone to a dinner party by saying "Hey! I'm hosting a meal for my mortal enemies and I immediately thought of you! Come!"

But there's a bigger consideration here, too. The word "troll" evokes a distant other. An ogre under a bridge. An inhuman monster who emerges from their dwelling to taunt the good, hardworking people of the village. But this is not how I see my guests. Or, at least, it is no longer how I see my guests. Frank is a man who has a dog named Cinnamon. He also called me a piece of shit. Josh is a teenager whose high school experience reminds me of my own. And, yes, he also said I was a moron. Anna is a teacher who, very relatably, deals with mental health issues. Anna also happens to find my videos condescending and off-putting. Matthew is a person who reminds me of myself, a queer liberal artist who finds ways to discuss social issues through his work. He also thought that I represented "some of the worst aspects of liberalism." And Adam is a college student, eager to start friendly conversations with strangers on the internet. And he has also been taught some very homophobic ideas.

My guests are more than what they have said about me, so how can I see them, these three-dimensional humans, as "trolls"? They don't live under a bridge. Their entire lives are not built around tormenting the villagers. On the contrary, they are *fellow* villagers. My conversations with them have rendered me incapable of using this word. And this isn't for some performative purity, or political correctness to the extreme, but for the simple fact that, now that I've spoken to them, I can't unsee their humanity.

"Forget them," I recall my well-meaning friends consoling me when I first began to receive the incoming messages and comments that would soon fill the HATE FOLDER. "They're all just sad, lonely guys who live in their mothers' basements."

At the time I had a hunch this wasn't true, but now I know it's just a convenient lie. Many of my guests lead robust social lives with healthy family bonds. Most belong to a community. And for those who do grapple with isolation or the economic inability to move out of their childhood homes, that only makes them more relatable.

But why have I decided to banish the word "troll" but not the word "hate"? Both, after all, are imprecise and hyperbolic. Both are used as oversimplified shorthand for complicated social interactions. Both are employed so freely, and have been so thoroughly normalized, that any detractor can be called a "troll" and any negativity gets the label "hate." So, why do I like one and not the other?

◎

It's the second weekend in August. I know that I should be finalizing the show's third episode; instead, though, I'm glued to my phone, refreshing it for updates in horror.

Self-identified white supremacists are marching in Charlottesville, Virginia. "You will not replace us!" they chant, tiki torches in hand. Some are openly flying flags emblazoned with the Nazi swastika. A former leader of the Ku Klux Klan is in attendance, and he seems thrilled at what he sees. "This represents a turning point for the people of this country," he says proudly in an interview.

In response, I see friends take strong and inspiring oppositional stances.

"Hate has no home here," some of them say defiantly.

But, I think to myself, *clearly it does.*

"This is not who we are!" digital acquaintances triumphantly shout.

Well, I silently respond, *it's apparently who some of us are.*

This is the time-honored American tradition where we, the Good People, see a horrific atrocity in the news and immediately distance ourselves from the assailant by calling them subhuman names like *monster* or *animal* or *loser* or *coward.*

"*That* is not us!" we shout. "We, over here, are Good and they, over there, are Bad."

These statements often give me goosebumps, and I have sometimes even joined in with the chorus. But seeing them today leaves a strange taste in my mouth. Not because the actions being condemned aren't atrocious. They are. Nor is it because I want to downplay the terror of white supremacy. It is, by definition, terrorizing. This strange taste, instead, comes from my uncomfortable awareness that we distance ourselves from those Bad People to uphold the image we've constructed of ourselves and our larger national community. Vehemently insisting that "hate has no home here," allows us to move on without any meaningful interrogation of the circumstances that led to the heinous actions happening in the first place. And this permits us to delay confronting the scariest truth of all: that dangerous ideologies and violent behaviors grow in *humans*. Which means, horrifyingly, that they can grow in us, too.

Finally, I see why I'm comfortable with the phrase "people who hate me" and not the word "trolls." One humanizes. The other dehumanizes. One acknowledges the complicated truth that it is real human beings who write negative things online, while the other lulls us into the fantasy that only inhuman monsters—distant ogres who live under a bridge— are responsible for this vitriol. And while it may feel good in the short run to linguistically banish my guests to a subterranean chamber, does it actually help anyone in the long run? As I've been discovering on each of my phone calls, my guests are not some human anomaly "over there." On the contrary, they and I are made up of the same stuff, however different outside influences on that stuff may be.

"That same seed that you are kind of carrying . . . they're carrying that seed differently," I recall telling Adam about the Westboro Baptist Church.

Maybe thinking of hate as a seed is not only for Adam, but for me, too. Maybe it is too binary to see ourselves as "hateful" or "not hateful." Maybe we are just soil. And how the seed of hate grows within us has a lot to do with how we nurture it and who we entrust as our fellow gardeners. Under the wrong care some seeds may sprout into an ugly and overt form of hatred, while for others it may bloom into a begrudging tolerance for those who are different from us. Others may harbor the seed unknowingly, and some, like Adam, may even mistake it for love.

Thankfully, hate is not the only type of seed. A question can be a seed, too. One that takes root in our minds and stays with us for as long as we choose to tend to it. Maybe it leads us to reconsider what we call "love." Maybe it sparks a careful interrogation of the words we use to define other people.

The cacophony of the internet makes it alarmingly easy to misinterpret all negativity as "hate." Between the natural dehumanization that comes with the game, the hyperbolic way we're encouraged to speak to each other, and the sheer volume of information that the Everything Storm makes us process every day, it is easy to mistakenly equate someone calling us "annoying" with a person who wants to see us dead. To falsely sort constructive criticism into a container for vitriol that also houses a stranger who called us a "piece of shit." But the banality of hate, the ease with which we can express it in an instant, and the confusion of what we misinterpret as "hate" online, further proves the value of conversation. That through talking to each other we can better define what is and isn't hate—and that through this connection we are able to identify a seed in someone else that they may not have noticed before.

5

debate is a sport

Well, I knew this day would come eventually.

I examine the HATE FOLDER the way a farmer might inspect a barren field, wondering where to harvest next. By now every member of the HATE FOLDER has either refused my invitation onto the show, not responded to my invitation at all, or I've disqualified them for an egregiously violent message. Of course, if they don't fit into one of those categories then they are one of the ten people with whom I've already recorded a conversation. So, as I sit on my metaphorical tractor, I rev the engine and prepare to find crops elsewhere. Luckily, I know just the spot.

One of my most popular videos at Seriously.TV was "Happy Heterosexual Pride Day," a fake PSA that I had made in response to the outcry from a small but vocal faction of straight people who saw gay pride and demanded a celebration of their own. In this direct-to-camera video I sat on a stool as soft instrumental music played beneath me and recounted the fake history of this fake holiday. Many found it to be hilarious. Luckily, others found it to be unfunny trash, which means that its comment section is the perfect place to find my next guest.

"Truly cancer," wrote one commenter.

"Shut up faggot," wrote another.

"? Why is this dumbass video on my timeline," asked a third.

Then, a fourth catches my eye. "KILLLLLLLLLLLLLLLLLLL-

LLLLLLL yourself you victim complex havin' bitch boi." The author employed twenty-three extra Ls for emphasis. "I love gay people but people like this, no matter their gender, race or sexuality, should be put on an island to die."

"Kill yourself," along with its many cousins, is a sadly frequent barb on social media. I have been told before to drink bleach, stop breathing, and, as a reference to my video series, unbox my suicide. I briefly consider my own rule that forbids me from interviewing anyone who has threatened me with physical violence, but as I've recently determined, messages like these get by on a technicality: This commenter is not vowing to hurt me. He is simply submitting a request that I do it myself.

By clicking on the author's hyperlinked name I am transported to a tightly cropped profile picture of a man looking just off-camera. His face is framed by a beard. His name is E. From what I can tell, E is Canadian.

"Hey E! I just saw your comment under my video. I see you're not a fan—lol . . . no worries, that's actually why I'm writing to you today. I make a podcast where I have extended conversations with people who write me comments like these. It's not to 'shut each other down' or even debate, only to talk so I can figure out where you were coming from and you can figure out where I'm coming from, too. Would you be interested in being a guest?" *Send.*

"I'd be down for This," E writes back immediately. "You sound very reasonable, I think I'd love to be on."

◎

Twelve days later I settle into my chair, tap the microphone suspended before me, and dial E's number.

"Heyoooo," E says after a couple rings, musically elongating his o's as if he is a beloved recurring sitcom character and this is his catchphrase.

There is something immediate and chemical about this tiny, mundane moment. A calm sets over me whenever I hear a guest's voice for the first time. It happens in every call. No matter how egregious the comment may have been, this initial greeting invariably fills me with a sense of warmth, and makes it seem like our animosity is a charade that we've simply decided to postpone.

Starting small, I ask how he's doing.

"I was going to go for, you know, apply for some jobs later," he replies. E, I learn, is heading into his second year at university, and is on the hunt for restaurant work. He's studying computer science and is in the middle of building a game that's like *Brick Breaker* but his version has "guns that shoot back at you, lasers and stuff."

"Are you a gamer or is this more just like a technical interest?" I ask, like some doting aunt trying to make conversation with her adult nephew at a holiday party.

"Yeah. I mean, I play games, yeah, mostly on my computer," E replies. His responses are brief and almost avoidant. I get it. Many guests usually take time to open up, so I try to keep an open ear in these first minutes of our call to gauge what they seem most interested in discussing.

"What do you like to do for fun?"

"Oh, I mean I play a little bit of guitar here and there. Just some doodling with friends every once in a while, smoke a little bit of weed."

"Nice!" I say, perhaps a little too eagerly, desperately trying to sound chill. "Which is legal for you guys, up in Canada, right?"

"No! It's not yet," he reports, and then proceeds to share his unfiltered thoughts on Justin Trudeau, Canada's "ponyboy prime minister," as E calls him. "He's probably going to hold on to that until the next election, I'm assuming, so people will vote for him again."

This sudden turn into political territory is the most animated I've heard E yet. So, eager to get this call rolling, and thinking that this will loosen him up, I initiate a brief detour into politics, which leads us to a rolling discussion of the following:

E's political identity ("generally" conservative), anti-Trump protests, the purpose of said protests in Canada ("like, he's not even our fucking president," E says with disdain), political tribalism, Charlottesville, how to correctly condemn the white supremacists who marched in Charlottesville, Antifa ("That's a real problem," E says. "They are basically akin to Nazis."), the modern media landscape, conspiracy theories, free speech, Canada's Human Rights Tribunals ("If you refuse to use someone's preferred pronouns," E warns, "they can fine you."), trans identity, Antifa again, Charlottesville again, confederate statues, the Civil War, whether or not a soldier should be held accountable for the actions of their commander, Trump again, racism, Trump round three, the Human Rights Tribunals again, gender pronouns again, the term *Orwellian*, whether or not we can use the term *Orwellian* if we've never read *1984* (neither of us have), biology, transracialism, chivalry, healthcare, mental healthcare, the concept of gender as a spectrum, our respective transgender friends, and finally—to top it all off—we have a tense exchange on whether or not we even have a right to talk about social issues that don't personally affect us.

By the time that we finally disengage from this charged back and forth, I look at the clock only to discover that this "brief" political detour lasted an entire forty-four minutes. Which, in addition to our opening small talk, now puts us one whole hour into our call. This is the entire time we had allotted to speak, and I fear that this recording is going to be unusable. I make a mental note to cut these forty-four minutes—that is, *if* this conversation even gets to the edit stage.

Mentally, I am out of breath, my brain silently wheezing on the sidelines. But this exhausting detour, while expansive and certainly chaotic, didn't exactly feel like the Everything Storm; the problem was less the volume of topics we discussed and more the *way* we were discussing them. The further it went on, the more combative we became. What happened? How did we get so far from our sweet conversation about E's job applications and video game designs?

I review these forty-four minutes in my head, replaying them in slow motion and as I do, I notice that I was combative, defensive, and, in many cases, the agitator, less listening to E and more devising ways to one-up him while he spoke. When E said something I considered to be offensive or wrong—like suggesting that enforcing gender pronouns was "Orwellian"—I was less interested in understanding *why* he felt this way and more focused on launching a devastating and funny retort. When he said Antifa was "basically akin" to Nazis, I had been so focused on workshopping a quippy rebuttal, that I didn't remember what he said after that. When he claimed that Canada's Human Rights Tribunals could fine people for misusing someone's gender pronouns, I was desperately mapping out a defense strategy in my head, but ultimately had to scrap it because I had never heard of these tribunals and didn't have the background information necessary to fight him on it.

Throughout these forty-four minutes I had been engaging him as if a scoreboard hung just above us and might light up in my favor if I said the right thing. And as the instant replay highlight reel continues to loop, I can see I wasn't having a conversation with E. I was trying to debate him.

◎

Debate has enjoyed a long and healthy life in high school extracurricular organizations, political spheres, and college campuses, but its rebirth as a modern form of entertainment is more recent. The documentary *Best of Enemies* pinpoints 1968 as its cultural revitalization when the broadcast network ABC hired two prominent writers to comment on the presidential election each night of the Republican and Democratic National Conventions. Gore Vidal, the acclaimed novelist and screenwriter, represented liberal thought, while William F. Buckley, founder of the *National Review*, represented the conservative perspective. Each night of the conventions the two men would spar with each other over their political disagreements, throwing verbal daggers from their chairs. This had never really been done on television before. Current events were primarily mediated through the calm and reassuring tone of solo news anchors who sat behind desks before stacks of paper, staring directly at the viewer through the camera. But this new format created a tense fireworks display of disagreement, and these nightly broadcasts drew millions of viewers, more than any other network.

Many believe that the explosive success of the Vidal and Buckley debates laid the foundation for the cable news punditry we see on television today, where each night oppositional voices scream at each other in tidy talking points. More recently, this format seems to have been reborn on YouTube where various opinion merchants post videos of themselves "destroying" their ideological foe—as advertised by photoshopped thumbnails that juxtapose close-ups of their cartoonish faces in various stages of exaggerated indignation.

It is precisely for this reason that I intentionally vowed to never make *Conversations with People Who Hate Me* into a debate show. I even explicitly stated this in the show's first episode. Nobly, I wanted to offer a new model of communication, a more loving alternative, and yet, here I find myself wiping off the theoretical sweat after my ideological scrimmage with E.

These forty-four minutes weren't a downpour from the Everything Storm, they were the natural consequence of being in the center of the Debate Arena. And now that I know where we are, it's my job to get us out.

$$\odot$$

"So, E," I say with an exhale, trying to start anew, "you wrote in a public comment—"

E recoils with what sounds like apprehension. He knows what's coming next.

"You said, 'KILLLLLLLLLLLLLLLLLLLLLLLLLLL yourself you victim complex havin' bitch boi. I love gay people but people like this, no matter their gender, race or sexuality, should be put on an island to die.'"

"Looking back at it, it wasn't the most informed or appropriate comment to make," he says. "On the topic of pride days in general, like gay pride, I think it's so sad the way they are now."

Strangely, a wave of relief comes over me. While I profoundly disagree with what he just said, we are finally disagreeing about something that I actually have the authority to discuss, rather than a distant current event that we are sparring about as bystanders.

"What they've all turned into is just a focus on being really, really eccentrically gay in the middle of the street," E says, elaborating on his opposition to pride celebrations. "It's kind of pointless as I . . . the way I see it right now."

"Yeah. And I don't see it as pointless," I reply, cautiously trying to express my disagreement while still resisting the gravitational pull

117

of the Arena. "I think the showy, entertaining things are a great and amazing part of the queer community, but also, just to be real, I wear high-waisted jeans and a long sleeve button-down shirt and a sweater on hot days—"

E laughs at this image.

"—and that's how *I* go to the parade. And I go with my husband and we're queer and we kiss there and it feels safe to kiss there."

E jumps in with a question: "Do you really feel like . . . let's say you're just . . . it's just an ordinary day. Do you really feel that afraid to kiss your husband?"

"One hundred percent," I say with a calm authority.

"Really?"

"One hundred percent."

"Has anything bad ever actually happened to you?" E presses. I can't tell if this is facetious skepticism or sincere curiosity, but I give him the benefit of the doubt and continue as if it is the latter.

"Yes," I say definitively.

"If you don't mind . . ." E says. And then, catching himself, he adds, "Actually, I'm not sure if it's just sad or traumatic for you but . . ." he trails off. Still, I know exactly what he is trying to say.

As has become frequent on these calls, I'm struck by the fact that the same person who had told me to kill myself, the very stranger who said that people like me "should be put on an island to die," is now delicately checking in to make sure that his curiosity doesn't re-traumatize me, while giving me space to not answer his question if it makes me uncomfortable. This moment would never have even been possible in the heated atmosphere of the Debate Arena.

"No, that's okay," I say, before recounting the numerous times that Todd and I have been threatened in public, telling E about all the looks we've gotten when holding hands. I narrate to E the first vacation I ever took with Todd—a road trip to Montreal—and recall how two separate cars threateningly revved their engines and lurched toward us as we passed them in crosswalks. And throughout all of these stories, E carefully listens.

"I feel like I've learned something now because I really didn't know that," he says genuinely.

Only an hour ago we were in the central ring of the Debate Arena, facing each other down, and now look at us. At the same time, I'm aware that I have yet to address his egregious opening line. Now that we've taken off our boxing gloves, I figure that this is the best chance I'll get.

"I am not bringing this up to scold you or anything," I begin, cautiously. "If I had seen this comment directed at me when I was really going through it as a teenager, this comment would have ruined me, right? Now, this is, unfortunately, something that I've grown a thick skin to, so I just scroll past it, you know?" As I say this, I visualize the younger me, the me who questioned whether it was worth existing at all, the me who might have interpreted a comment like "kill yourself" as proof that I didn't really belong in this world, perhaps even as a directive. I assume that I'm going to keep this memory private, but then, surprising even myself, I speak it aloud: "I never attempted it, but I always entertained that idea. That's how low I felt as a kid."

I leave this memory hanging out in the open space between us, suspended in the void. I'm not sure how he'll take it, or what he'll say in response.

There is a flash of silence, and then E enters it.

"I'd rather not go into the specifics, but I—" he begins, catching himself. "There was a time in my life, I was fourteen or whatever, and I would almost kind of try to kill myself."

His confession renders me momentarily speechless. It hangs in the air alongside mine, our floating vulnerabilities now meeting each other somewhere in the digital telephone wires that connect our voices. We have unlocked these forgotten memory chambers—not through quips, or talking points, or rebuttals, but by a slowly built mutual trust. And now that we've found a rhythm, we seamlessly glide into explorations of our respective childhoods, narrating to each other who we were as kids and who we are now. We trade our different definitions of strength. There is no scoreboard here, I am no longer drafting sharp retorts. We are locked in a fluid back and forth of questions and answers. Finally, we are dancing.

"Do you regret writing that comment?" I ask.

"I would say I definitely regret making that comment. After watching the whole video and definitely hearing some of the things that you've told me in terms of your experience as a gay man, I definitely regret most of the meaning behind it. Obviously, in terms of the 'Kill yourself,' and the 'on an island to die' were never meant to be serious in the first place. It was certainly more passing, like, 'Fuck off,' kind of a thing."

"Yeah. So, I'll cancel my trip to that island," I joke.

"It's not very nice anyways," E says back. "The beaches there are gross."

I smile. "Well, E, thank you so much for taking the time to talk with me," I say, wrapping up the call. "I hope you have a great day, and I'll see you on the internet, okay?"

"Thank you. You, too. It's been great. Thanks a lot for having me."

I hang up the phone, still sore from our jabs in the Debate Arena, but soaring from the connection we were able to forge at the end. If the second half of this two-hour call with E was a collaborative waltz, then the first half was a far more competitive endeavor. If conversation is a dance, then debate, I now see, is a sport.

We love debate for the same reason we love sports: It satisfies our itch to firmly declare a winner and loser at the end of a battle. And who can blame us? We live in an era when prestige is gained through obliterating, destroying, owning, and dunking on our opponent. Social media platforms promise us bountiful hauls of gold coins if we do it well. Conveniently, the very design of these social media platforms flattens other human beings into two-dimensional avatars, making it all the easier to see our enemies—or perceived enemies— not as fellow people, but bullseyes on which we can perfect our aim. We believe that this is noble target practice, the most productive way we can fight for our beliefs. And by perfecting our aim, we tell our- selves, we can win.

But what does winning a debate actually do? Does it change minds? Does it advance social justice causes? That would be lovely if so, but I worry that it is more of a performance for those who have already made up their minds. An opportunity to impress those who already agree with us. Thinking back to my scrimmage with E, what would dunking on him actually have accomplished? Would he have instantaneously agreed with all of my views on trans identity? Would he have magically been transformed into an ally who lists his pro- nouns in his bio? Or would he have just felt bad for a moment before continuing to believe what he already believed? I have never changed my long-held beliefs because someone humiliated me with a good joke. Nor have I switched political parties because the candidate from the other side came up with a better quip. Like athletic dominance, winning a debate may feel good in the moment, but I don't know if it effects actual change. And seeing debate as a sport is also a helpful way to understand its limits.

Just as sports don't work without rules, debate doesn't work without a shared understanding of facts. The very premise of a "fair debate" falls apart when a truth can be trumped by a total lie. If, for example, one person says, "climate change is caused by carbon emissions," and the rebuttal from the other side is "actually, climate change doesn't even exist," then there's no debate to be had. The opposing sides need to, at the very least, agree on the existence of the topic they are there to debate. And that's a challenge because facts are having a tricky time these days. For one thing, the age of information overload—the Everything Storm itself—feeds us the illusion that all is knowable, but it isn't possible to be an expert on every relevant subject because a new subject is deemed "relevant" every second. A general debate becomes challenging in an era when the word "general" means everything, ever. Additionally, we are living at a time when disinformation and misinformation run rampant. Sure, every fact can be corroborated by a Google search, but so too can every nonfact. To have a debate without a shared pool of facts is like trying to play basketball against baseball, so chaotic that it immediately renders the activity pointless. There were many moments in my forty-four-minute detour into the Debate Arena with E when I wished we had a researcher. *Do* the Canadian Human Rights Tribunals indeed fine people for using the wrong pronouns? What is Antifa *really*? We couldn't have an honest debate about any of these topics without a common understanding of the truth behind them.

Sports are not built to explore complicated interpersonal dynamics or sensitive social issues. They are, however, terrific methods to determine absolute outcomes: winners, losers, and MVPs. Debate offers the same function. It can be a helpful practice to identify the strongest orator, determine which side formed the best argument, and which team deserves the trophy. Just like sports, though, debate is not the ideal venue in which to process complicated topics that require empathy and listening and time. Topics like identity. I was uncomfortable when the subject of trans issues came up with E, not because we shouldn't discuss complex topics that some don't yet understand, but because I don't believe that marginalized identities should be debated or fought over. Instead, I believe they should be processed and understood with care. Additionally, neither E nor I are trans, and, as I had been learning from the frequency with which Black Lives Matter would come up on calls when no one on the call was Black, there is little value in having an argument about a social movement when both participants lack the personal experience necessary to validate such an argument with a stamp of legitimacy. When sensitive social issues like identity are broached, the discussion becomes too abstract and it often devolves into a friend-off, where participants determine who has more expertise through proximity. To debate something as nuanced as identity is like trying to settle a delicate marital rift through a game of dodgeball.

Ultimately, though, debate is gamified conversation. Like sports, it is entertainment, a spectacle of opposition. Both are played to an audience, and both create an adversarial dynamic between those involved. They reward devastating clapbacks and dunks over the far more boring actions of listening and sharing. Sure, I suppose it would have been entertaining if E and I duked it out on any of the topics that were thrown our way. Perhaps a heated back and forth about the merits and demerits of Antifa, an explosive argument about President Trump, or even a roast battle about free speech could have been the powder keg we needed to explode into a screaming match, but none of these approaches would have allowed me to truly get to know him.

I can tune in to any cable news show to find a pundit reciting their workshopped talking points, I can watch politicians debate if I need to get my kicks, and there is a new YouTube drama to follow every day, but those will never allow me to ask Josh why he called me a "moron" and learn about how he struggled to get by in high school. I could go head-to-head with Frank about our political disagreements but I would never have learned what made him a conservative. And I could rehearse the most devastating clapbacks and hone my most clever talking points, but I would never find out what fourteen-year-old E had in common with fourteen-year-old Dylan.

Conversation is, I believe, the best alternative. Unlike debate, conversation is not something that can be won. To pursue such an outcome would be like trying to dominate at compromise, demolish at understanding, or absolutely crush at empathizing. Debate may look like conversation from far away, but up close, it becomes immediately apparent that the two are made up of completely different material. If the fundamental building blocks of debate are statements and rebuttals, then conversations are composed of questions and responses. It was through asking each other questions, and genuinely wanting to hear the answers, that E and I were able to sow seeds of curiosity, redirecting our battle into a dance. Dance enables us to find out about our partner, whereas debate demands that we crush our opponent. Even those verbs tell completely different stories: *finding* versus *crushing*. Discovery versus destruction.

In debate, as in sports, vulnerability is synonymous with weakness. In conversation, however, it's a strength. Vulnerability is, in fact, the skeleton key that opens the doors of distant memory chambers, it is the most direct pathway out of the Debate Arena, it is the beat that underscores the dance.

Any two strangers can fight, but we must feel safe before dancing with someone. And the safer we feel, the more comfortable we are to let our partner in, to share more about ourselves, to unlock our secret memory chambers that even we were surprised to open. And it is in these hidden rooms that we can find the context that the internet erases, the backstory that social media obscures, and the human being freed from their online avatar.

◉

Now that the podcast is up and running, people who haven't listened to the show but know its central premise will praise me for hosting a debate show. "That's what we're missing these days!" they'll often say as they clasp my shoulders. "Healthy debate! Good on you for doing it." And then they'll give me a strong pat on the back like a proud coach throwing a player into the game. At first this bothered me, and made me want to devise newer, louder ways to announce my mission. *Conversations with People Who Hate Me: NOT a Debate Show!!!!* I briefly imagine the new logo screaming, the added disclaimer bigger than the title itself. But the more this happens, the more I'm coming to understand that maybe these kind, well-meaning supporters aren't misunderstanding the show as much as they're revealing that "debate" is the only word we know to use for conversations across disagreement. And because of this, debate becomes our default.

Of course, I understand the desire to spar with our ideological opponents as it ensures a healthy distance between us and our adversaries. Because when we engage them in conversation, that distance shortens. And as that distance shortens, we begin to feel a kinship with the very people we once wrote off as enemies. And then, the strangest thing happens: We start to empathize with them.

6

empathy is not endorsement

New England whizzes past my window, its trees showing off their new autumnal colors. Unfortunately, I can't appreciate any of them because I am hunched over my laptop pressing my headphones into my ears to drown out the mechanical screeching of the train, as I try to do a final-pass listen of the final mix for what might be the final episode of *Conversations with People Who Hate Me*. After nine episodes I feel ready for a break. Or an end. I'm not quite sure. This project has been more taxing than I imagined and I'm trying to figure out how I can continue making it. But I put that out of my mind because I don't want to think about the future. Right now, I'm focused on this final episode. In the present.

It is October 1, 2017, and I'm riding the Acela back from Boston after a weekend with Todd, who is now in his second year of law school. Just eleven months ago, on this same train going the opposite direction, I had quickly typed a half-baked idea for a creative project that would connect adversarial strangers. It's a bittersweet, full-circle moment and I'm already feeling pangs of nostalgia. I'll miss the weekly cadence of releasing a new piece of work, but most of these pangs come from a surprising place: Deep down, I am going to really miss my guests.

Once I finish listening to the episode, I look out the window. We're already in Rhode Island and, as Providence approaches, I wonder how my guests are at this very moment. How is Adam doing back at school? Did E find that restaurant job? How is Frank's dog, Cinnamon? And, of course, I wonder about Josh. He's been with me since the beginning, since that first train ride in the opposite direction nearly a year ago, when, in the wake of the election I was contemplating my next move. I had no idea on that first call a seed was being planted in my head, that that seed would sprout into a whole project, and I had no idea about all the people I'd get to know because of it. I regard Josh the way one might a younger brother. He's finally out of high school. Does he feel as free as he imagined he would?

But these warm feelings also come with a familiar knot. An asterisk on all of these wholesome sentiments of friendship. I really, really like my guests and think about them often. Also, many hold views that I profoundly disagree with. How can I reconcile these two truths? How is it possible to really like the people I was speaking to, to empathize with these strange and wonderful new friends, while also deeply disagreeing with some of their beliefs?

There is, at this moment in time, a widespread push to *resist*. The word and its varied iterations are emblazoned on bumper stickers, protest signs, merch, and social media profiles. The idea being that we on the left must resist all that comes with this new administration. But the vagueness of the phrase prompts questions. Resist what exactly? Authoritarianism? Heck yeah! White supremacy? For sure. Empathy for people who think differently from us? Oh. Maybe that, too? As is common with still-burgeoning cultural movements, the rules remain unclear as they're being drafted in the public square. Everyone seems to be interpreting the concept in their own way. Some friends have blocked family members on social media, others have severed ties with childhood friends, and a few people I know have been taking to social media to shame any hint of humanization of any member of the other side. Forgiveness seems to be a sin. Kindness a thing of the past. This is war. Or rather, this is *resistance.* The word itself implies temptation. It hints at an inherent challenge. After all, you don't resist dental surgery, you resist sugar. Was seeing my conservative guests as human some sort of ideological treason?

As the train glides toward New York City, and the hours close in before the final episode is released, I come to terms with the silence I'm about to face when this project pauses. Or ends. I'm still not quite sure. Either way, there will be a void. And in this void I will have to face down the ethical questions that have been plaguing me. Am I doing something wrong by empathizing with my guests? Is this something I should be resisting? Are harmful ideologies contagious? Did my empathy act as a sort of permission slip for my guests to continue believing what they already believed? By treating them as human, was I cosigning every one of their political beliefs?

My mind whirls with shoulds and should nots; it echoes with the voices of my perceived critics through an amplification system of my own insecurities. It is my own little personal Everything Storm, wailing with the ambiguities left in the wake of a too-broad mandate. How can I balance what my guests believe with who I know them to be from our conversations? Luckily, I remember that I've found myself in a similar predicament before.

◎

For many years after college I worked in the service industry. First as a cashier at a gourmet grocery store, then as a barista at a celebrity-infested New American restaurant, later as a server at that restaurant, and eventually, when I couldn't handle another supermodel indignantly refusing my third request that she extinguish her cigarette, I walked my résumé a few blocks over to a small, beloved vegan restaurant where each day felt like a new *Portlandia* sketch.

I loved this work very much. My days would fly by since time was not marked by minutes, but rather a steady stream of customers who, simply by existing before me, opened up a small window into their lives, even if only for a fleeting moment. All of them just feeling their feelings and, to varying degrees, using me as a receptacle for those feelings. Within one hour I might be a confidant to the local gallery owner, a sentient coffee machine to the ad executive who lived across the street, a captive audience member for a regular customer's impromptu open mic, or a punching bag for the renowned columnist who regarded all of us as his personal staff. My job was to receive whatever they sent my way, while silently taking their orders, honoring their tailored requests, and treating them as royalty I was lucky to serve, all while knowing that forty minutes after our exchange, most would likely forget that I even existed.

Some customers were wonderful; the vast majority were benign and forgettable, but it is the bad customers that I'll remember until my last breath. In the same way that there are some social media interactions that make me want to throw my phone into the deepest chasm of hell, sell all of my earthly possessions, and join a screen-free farming cult in rural Maine, there were customer exchanges that made me dream of dramatically ripping off my apron, setting it on fire, and delivering an impassioned monologue about proletariat resistance before rage-quitting in a blaze of glory.

Unfortunately, I needed money to pay rent and feed myself. Fortunately, my roommate tipped me off to a helpful coping mechanism.

In my first year in the service industry, I lived with my college friend Nomi in an apartment where we traded such luxury items as "windows" and "fresh air" for cheaper rent. She was my rock throughout that year, often there to console me after a rough shift. One day when I was regaling her with an account of the way some monster masquerading as a human being ordered an omelette, she sighed and said, "Well, hurt people hurt people." The phrase landed within me like a small poem. It was a puzzle I needed to do right then and there. *Hurt people hurt people.* The first "hurt" was an adjective, the second was a verb. It was a shockingly succinct way to distill the cyclical nature of harm.

Immediately, I applied the phrase retroactively to a customer I remembered from the grocery store. I recalled how she was frantically detailing the very specific set of requirements that needed to be met before I rang up her items. The scanner, she stipulated, needed to be covered. The lasers, she explained, couldn't touch her food. This meant that I needed to ring up her items manually by punching in the long codes, digit by digit. That wasn't all. Surgical gloves needed to be worn, specific cleaning solution needed to be pre-sprayed on the counter, and, oh, by the way she also couldn't be in close proximity to any fellow shoppers wearing perfume.

Hurt people hurt people, I reminded myself. This woman, I mused, must have suffered from extreme anxiety. Or she had high-level, top secret government intel that was telling her to stay away from lasers. Either way, she was carrying a heavy burden and I understand why it might have been easier to momentarily share it with whomever happened to be nearby.

When I took this phrase with me to the New American restaurant, I found that it didn't only work with customers, but my bosses, too. I was a barista at the restaurant when a high-powered celebrity couple came in with their children. The restaurant's overseer, who typically worked remotely, came into the restaurant that day so that she could greet them herself. Once they arrived, she graciously showed them to their table, cracking jokes along the way. And the next thing I knew she was charging toward me. "Make me a babycino," she commanded through gritted teeth. By this point I had been well-schooled in the art of coffee through the mandatory training the restaurant required. I knew how to pull a perfect espresso shot, steam the milk so precisely that it became silk, and over time I was able to make those little leaves of latte art. But never throughout my entire training had I ever heard the ungodly term *babycino*. Surely it was a made-up drink only served in those boutiques that sell couture toddler overalls by appointment. I had no idea what she was talking about. *What is a babycino?* Unfortunately, I made the mistake of daring to ask her this question out loud. Once those four words left my mouth, she looked at me in horror, as if I had just confessed to murdering her entire family.

"It's chocolate milk, foamed with a dusting of cocoa powder on top," she replied as if I was the stupidest person alive for not knowing that. "Please make me a babycino. Right. Now." The way her tongue hit the "t" of "right" is the stuff of nightmares. I think I blacked out because all I can remember is her grabbing the drink from my hands while I was still reeling from the fact that I was on the brink of losing my job because I didn't know how to make a drink that didn't exist.

Even then, I breathed and reminded myself: *Hurt people hurt people.* My boss was a woman in the male-dominated restaurant world and needed to get ahead however she could. If that meant staying in the good graces of celebrities by serving their spawn made-up drinks, then I accepted my position as her punching bag.

I was months into being a server when I began a brunch shift in the restaurant's upstairs dining room, setting up tables for the day ahead. Typically, guests would first be seated downstairs, giving me ample time to prep the upstairs dining room. So, while I was doling out servings of jam into ramekins I was surprised to see two five-year-old boys sprint up the staircase, trailed by someone who seemed to be their father. If I could describe this man in one word it would be *golf*. He was at least dressed for the sport. The maître d' followed them with three menus in her hand and before she could bring him to a table he said, "That," pointing to a booth usually reserved for parties of eight or more. Clearly wanting to be done with him, she obliged. He was now my problem. As he sat down, his sons clearly mistook this empty dining room for an indoor trampoline palace built just for them. As they ran around, I tried to extract an order from him, but instead of looking at the menu, he just rattled off words associated with breakfast. He ordered the waffles we didn't have, the fried chicken sandwich that was only available at dinner, and a dish that didn't even qualify for our cuisine. Eventually he caved and glanced at the menu, ordering plates for the table. Once delivered, the contents of these plates, which most people might eat, became the projectiles that his two children launched at each other from opposite sides of the dining room. The extra butter he demanded became the rubber bullets whose shrapnel was quickly embedded in the restored wood floors and the ramekins of jam were reimagined as cannonballs. The whole time he didn't look up from his phone or even try to stop his children from assaulting every piece of furniture the restaurant owned. And the whole time I shielded myself from the unfriendly fire that rang out.

Hurt . . . people . . . hurt . . . people. I struggled to even think the words, let alone speak them. Maybe some horrible tragedy rendered him a single parent and the task of balancing his grief with his newfound parental duties became too overwhelming and now all he can do is stare at his phone while his kids find whatever joy they can. *Yes*, I repeated to myself as I exhumed hardened jam from a tabletop across the room, *hurt people hurt people.*

This phrase quickly became the only way I could make it through the day without starting a workers' rebellion. It was a crucial exercise that allowed me to find even an infinitesimal sliver of them to love so that I could feed myself, pay the next month's rent, and then, when the time came, even be half honest when I looked them in the eye to say, "Have a nice day." These were fantasies I would weave in my mind, fictional backstories that allowed me to empathize with them. Then one day, I didn't have to imagine anymore.

Customers at the vegan restaurant were, for the most part, well-meaning people who were just looking to eat their plant-based meals in peace. Some left us pamphlets on the horrors of leather, others passed along books about the impending destruction of the planet through meat farming, but most just wanted to order a delicious meal and then go about their lives. These patrons were kind, and if they weren't particularly kind, they were at least quirky enough to be entertaining. I knew most of them by name and had a place in my heart for all of them.

Unfortunately, this meant that the mean customers became even more memorable. One woman had a deceptively kind face and looked like she could be the grandmother in an L.L. Bean catalog—modeling a fleece pullover on page 22 and reading under a cozy plaid blanket on pages 38 to 39. But this cozy image was quickly shattered when I first waited on her. As I poured her water and set her table, she glared at me the entire time, squinting her eyes in disgust as if I was a cockroach who managed to secure gainful employment at this dining establishment. Before I could tell her about the specials she barked her order at me, and then looked away as if doing so rendered my existence obsolete. Maybe, I told myself, she was just having a bad day. But this behavior was her norm. Maybe she just doesn't like me, I mused, but I soon observed her treating my colleagues this way, too.

Then, one evening she came in with a guest. I had only ever seen her alone and now she was here with a man who looked to be her partner. I went in with an open mind, hoping that perhaps she would treat me with a little more dignity now that she had a witness but upon arriving at their table, they snatched the menus from my hands and growled in unison. When it came time to order their meals, they barked their orders just as she always had when she was alone. The dining room was small enough that throughout their meal I was always in earshot of their conversation. Though, it was less a conversation and more a one-way monologue of the man berating her, snarling at her in the same way she spoke to us. I caught glimpses of her cowering in subordination, silently taking his vitriol. Now she was the cockroach. It was my first time seeing her like this, and I felt for her. *Hurt people hurt people* was on display right in front of me: The mean customer who berated me, only to be berated by her husband in the same exact way. Pain is the gift that keeps on giving, and if I was craving proof of the phrase's legitimacy, this would be Exhibit A.

Truthfully, I had understood the concept long before I knew the slogan. As an effeminate, clearly closeted, late bloomer I was bullied in high school. It wasn't the bullying from television, but rather that kind of surreptitious bullying that those of us who attended "accepting" schools in the early 2000s know well. We weren't stuffed in lockers; we were iced out of social gatherings instead. We weren't called "faggots"; we were just repeatedly asked if we were gay by the boys who were "Just checking. Damn, chill." And instead of being overtly sidelined we felt a constant dull sensation that we didn't quite belong. But don't worry, I was told repeatedly, everything was "just a joke." Like the times when my high voice was mocked, or when they said, "Ladies first," and gestured for me to lead the way, or when an older boy asked to take a picture with me and pulled his athletic cup out of his underwear and held it over my face as the camera snapped a picture, freezing my humiliation in celluloid amber for the rest of eternity. And because all of these moments were "Just jokes," I forced whatever laugh I could muster as often as I could.

But the harder the fake laugh, the more I was filled with a shame that I didn't yet have the words to describe. A variant of humiliation so complicated, and buried so deep, that it wound up emerging somewhere else entirely.

Sometimes I would get home and pick a fight with my mom for her crime of asking about my day. Other times I would explode at her for reminding me about a chore I had to do, transposing my daily pain into a nightly eruption. She, of course, deserved none of this. But I continued to bottle up the hurt, carefully compress it with the precision of a bomb squad, and then detonate it in front of her. Hurt people do, in fact, hurt people. Or, more accurately, hurt people hurt the people that they can get away with hurting.

Restaurants, high school, and social media all offer easy, lower-status punching bags for those looking to take their anger out on someone else. Servers become low-hanging fruit for customers who are having a bad day. Internet personalities can seem like convenient receptacles for vitriolic insults because there's a low probability that those insults will ever reach them. And high school, with its built-in hierarchy of age and popularity, allows those with more clout to pick on those with less—a convenient emotional release in a time when our hormones are raging, bodies are changing, and we don't yet have the verbal or emotional tools to express how we feel.

◎

The train is now crossing over from Connecticut to New York. *Hurt people hurt people*, I tell myself, hoping that this salve will help me now just as it did then. But it doesn't have the same effect as it did years ago in restaurants. It doesn't soothe my unease. *Hurt people hurt people* does nothing to placate the fear that I'm committing some ideological transgression by fostering connections with people from "the other side." Sure, it's a beautiful sentiment that poetically gets at a psychological truth, and, yeah, there are some parallels between my relationship with my guests and my relationships with my former customers, but I never thought I was committing a cultural sin by empathizing with cruel restaurant patrons. I was just trying to survive the day. Here it feels like a social sin to simply see them as human beings. It's as if I've pulled out a miracle ointment from the depths of the medicine cabinet, only to discover that it expired.

For one thing, the phrase isn't necessarily true for all of my guests. It's true for *some* of them. Josh took the bullying he endured at school and aimed it at me. Yet, neither Frank nor E had such a clear line from the hurt they had been dealt to the words they dealt me. Adam didn't even think he was hurting me at all. He thought he was saving me. Does it make it worse if they *weren't* hurt themselves?

There's also a difference in intention. At my restaurant jobs I was *trying* to empathize with my customers through fictional backstories that I forced myself to create, whereas here the empathy was just happening as if it was my body's automatic reaction to speaking with them. Like sweating during exercise. And to be fair, that's kind of what it was. Empathy, I'm learning, is a natural byproduct of talking to people. It is impossible when having a conversation to not see the other person as a three-dimensional human being, full of nuance and complexity. I didn't intend to empathize with them; it just sort of happened, less a saintly marvel and more a mundane inevitability.

"There isn't anyone you couldn't love once you've heard their story." I had frequently shared this quote—attributed to the Benedictine nun Sister Mary Lou Kownacki and popularized by Mister Rogers—but now here I am contending with the surprising aftertaste of its consequences. The questions pick up again. Did liking my guests affirm every one of their beliefs? Did feeling for them make me susceptible to their ideologies? Could I separate them, the individual person, from the movements that they were unknowingly part of? Was I enabling dangerous ideologies by genuinely liking and empathizing with the people who held them? Is it even possible to truly hold them accountable for what they said without pinning the sins of the system entirely on them?

I recall that recurring feeling I had with each of my guests. That moment when I separated Josh from homophobia, when Frank no longer became conservatism. When E was no longer the barb he had written to me. When Adam ceased to be all of dogmatic religious teachings. It was through the simple act of speaking with them that I was able to separate the person from their beliefs. This separation didn't absolve them of what they said to me, but it helped put it in perspective.

I imagine my guests as trees, and their respective ideologies as the forests to which they belong. From a distance we can only see the forest, and up close we can only see the tree. Social media makes that distance especially large. The digital public square only allows us to see the bigger picture, largely due to the sheer volume of trees we pass by every day; because of this, we miss the complexity of each individual tree. Intimate, one-on-one conversation is the antidote to social media because it allows us to see the bark up close. The intricate root systems, the interwoven canopies of leaves. Of course, then the opposite can happen: We can get caught up in the hyperspecificity of each tree and miss out on the larger patterns of the forest.

I'm now realizing that my biggest job in this project is to not lose sight of either. To hold both at the same time. To remember that the person I'm speaking to is not the harmful ideology they subscribe to, just as a tree is not the entire forest. Part of it, yes, but not all of it.

My real problem isn't with Josh or Frank or E or Adam. My real problem is with the woods of homophobia, the forest of conservatism. I really, really liked the trees I was talking to. But I really, really didn't like the forest. Of course, you can't have a conversation with a problematic interpretation of a religion. I couldn't call up homophobia, nor could I sit down with conservatism. Instead, I was left only with the tree. The representative. The person.

Just as *hurt people hurt people* helped me through customer service, I wish there were a tidy, concise phrase that I could carry in my pocket now. And then, I remember that one week into the podcast's release when I was wrestling with this very predicament, I had written a mantra for myself. I pull out my phone to find it, swiping past grocery lists, work-related to-do's, gift ideas, and nonsensical reminders, when I finally see what I had written: *Empathy is not endorsement.*

Yes, I think. *That's it.*

Empathizing with someone is the simple acknowledgment that they, like you, are a human. Empathizing with someone does not suddenly permit them to say and do awful things. People will do those things and think those things whether you empathize with them or not. Empathizing with someone does not cast a vote for their candidate. Only they can do that. Empathizing with someone doesn't turn their beliefs into a contagion. All this time that I had spent worrying that such a thing was possible that I failed to look at the person who would have been patient zero: me.

Yes, I see Josh as a brother, but that did not cause me to suddenly believe that being gay was a sin. I have warm feelings for Frank, but I did not change my political registration. I feel for Adam, but I do not suddenly see my sexuality as an addiction that can be cured. And I loved getting to know E, but that doesn't mean I suddenly became him. The empathy I felt for my guests was a natural byproduct of getting to know them.

But empathy is more than just a consequence of conversation; it's the necessary fuel that conversation needs to keep going. It is the signal of safety that allows two people to continue opening up to each other. It is insulation that makes my guests feel safe enough to share things with me. When any of us feel attacked we naturally put up our defenses, but when we find our rhythm, get out of the Everything Storm, see past the labels we've placed on each other, and avoid debate, we begin to finally open up, to show ourselves. To be vulnerable. And that's exactly what happened: Empathy gave my guests a more loving space to explore why they had written to me what they did, and, in turn, it gave both of us a window into another experience.

Empathy and hurt are both renewable resources. Just as hurt begets hurt, empathy begets empathy, too. And just as *hurt people hurt people* gave me exactly what I needed years earlier, *empathy is not endorsement* is the balm I need now.

I am grateful that Past Me had written down this mantra for Today Me, as if I had known that when this was all over the whispers would start, the doubt would creep in, and the fear would take over. As if he knew that this was the permission slip I would need to keep going. I don't know what Future Me will think of this mantra. I don't know how the future world will regard this project. I don't even know what I'm going to do next.

Right now all I can see is the New York City skyline approaching, as I breathe a little easier resting on this mantra that I've created. My very own pocket-sized reminder that is trying to tell me: *Keep going.*

7

empathy is a luxury

Mantras are lovely. They serve as helpful guideposts on the journey to the people we are becoming, the people we want to be. But without action, mantras are empty. So, if I want to continue exploring how empathy is, in fact, not the same thing as endorsement, then I should keep having conversations. I just need to figure out how.

It's mid-October. Fall's chill is just beginning to set into the New York City air, and I'm riding a surge of confidence after re-reading notes from listeners. A teacher told me that she used the show in her classroom as a template for her students to have their own difficult conversations. Many have thanked me for helping them speak to oppositional family members. A number of supporters have praised me for my bravery. But it's the note from a conservative listener that serves as my biggest fuel to keep going.

"I think what you are doing is amazing," the man wrote. "I have never found anyone, I mean anyone, that has your points of view and could have a calm and respectful conversation." Even now, months after receiving it, I savor this message, puffing up with a sense of pride that my work is actually reaching my political opposites, that I have finally built a project that invites everyone to the table.

Conversation, I have come to believe, is activism. And with the support of my listeners—and the blessing from this unlikely fan—I am ready to evangelize the good word of dialogue across division to all of the internet's billions of users.

The HATE FOLDER has been exhausted of options for a while now and I would rather not have to continue mining my inbox for homophobic taunts or re-scouring months-old comment sections with the hopes of finding a stranger's declaration that I'm the ugliest person that ever existed. Luckily, I have an idea of how to expand this project.

For the last few months I've quietly been nursing a fantasy: What if, instead of only speaking to my own detractors, I start moderating conversations between strangers who clashed with each *other* online? In this new format I see myself acting more as a host, creating a space for two digital enemies to come together and talk. The idea has excited me from the beginning, but it also makes sense as the next logical iteration of this project. For one thing, I am not the only person to have received hate online and I want others to experience the beauty of these conversations for themselves. What's more, I've gotten so much out of speaking to my own detractors that I'm now ready to help others do the same.

Luckily, I don't think I'll have a hard time finding participants. Recipients of online vitriol seem to frequently repost the hate comments they receive as a way to reclaim them. Sometimes these reposts are accompanied by pithy captions, devastatingly unbothered emojis, or earnest hashtags employed ironically.

"Sorry about it sis," an acquaintance might say in a public response to a body-shaming Instagram comment, perhaps with the emoji of a hand painting its fingernails in place of a period.

"Can't wait," I've seen a stranger bite back in a YouTube comment informing them that they're going to hell. They finished it off: "#bornthisway."

Others might repost a typo-riddled tweet from a political opponent and simply caption it "*their" to assert grammatical dominance.

This inclination to reclaim online hate through reposting—the revenge-through-retweet approach—is one I know quite well. I had been in that exact same spot one year earlier, when digitally dunking on my detractors seemed like the best possible retribution, and a pile of digital coins was the only consolation prize that might heal the indescribable hurt caused by a negative comment. But I also know that these quips and coin hauls only help for a brief moment because once the dopamine high wears off, we are only left with our pain.

Throughout this last year I have found conversation to be a much healthier alternative. It provides healing not through likes, but through a sort of digital restorative justice that may not have the same immediate satisfaction of a viral joke, but whose benefits last far, far longer. After sacrificing myself as the guinea pig in this social experiment, I'm confident that others will jump at the opportunity to do the same.

This updated format, however, comes with fresh challenges, as I now will need to reach out to two participants, which I begin to distinguish as *primary guests* and *secondary guests*. The recipients of the negativity and the authors of the negativity, respectively.

I begin by making a list of potential primary guests, which ends up being a collection of every friend, digital acquaintance, and public figure I know who has likely received online hate. It's an impressive roster of activists, comedians, writers, and actors so diverse that I can't contain my excitement about how varied and wonderful each of their conversations will be. Finally, this new format will allow the show to explore other social ills like anti-Black racism, transphobia, misogyny, Islamophobia, anti-Semitism, ableism, and so many others now that it isn't just me speaking to my own critics.

My mind runs wild as I fantasize about the celebrated writer finding his Josh and how beautiful their dance will be. I imagine how that activist will feel when she gets on the phone with her Frank, and how I'll be there every step of the way as they weather their own Everything Storm. I can almost hear the actor speaking to his Adam, and I savor the thought of them planting seeds of questions in each other's minds. I can perfectly picture that local organizer on the phone with their E, and how I'll escort them both to the quickest route out of the Debate Arena should they find themselves trapped there.

As I draft a plan of attack, a full orchestra assembles in my eardrums and these microscopic musicians raise their instruments to play the classic *Mission: Impossible* theme as I imagine my next steps.

The flutes start by trilling the song's iconic opening and we cut to:

Me, at my desk. It is midday and I am hunched over a laptop. The camera circles me as I furiously type out invitations to potential primary guests.

Within seconds, my computer begins to chime with replies. "Yes, Dylan" and "Count me in" and "You know it, bud" all populate the screen.

Next, I am in the back seat of a speeding cab, the orchestra in full swing, and I open the taxi door before gingerly stepping out onto smooth pavement. The camera glides with me into the restaurant where I greet a renowned activist who is waiting at a table; a protest sign lies at her feet. We smile and laugh but then our faces get serious because we are here to Do Work.

She whips out her phone and emphatically points to a hate message of her own, identifying a potential secondary guest.

Hmm, my squinting eyes suggest in a close-up shot.

What do you think? the activist's raised brow asks wordlessly.

"Let's do this," I'll say, in a deep movie star voice that I do not have.

"All right," chimes the activist.

Together we inhale, nod to each other, speedily draft an invitation, and then press send.

The invitation—which, for cinematic purposes, is visually represented as a sheet of translucent text—takes flight in the air, and the camera follows it from the activist's phone to the nearby Wi-Fi router, through an impossibly long maze of Ethernet cables, and then, finally, to the home of its intended recipient.

Smash cut to: A nightstand. A phone lies face-up. The screen illuminates with a notification and a hand comes in frame to check it. There is a close-up on this person's face, their glowing phone is reflected in their pupils, which anxiously dart back and forth. Sweat beads form at the bridge of their nose.

"What the—" they'll say, but they're abruptly cut off for dramatic effect. (Also, this is a family film.)

The next scene takes place days later as the activist and I adjust our microphones. The frame is then cut into two halves, creating a split-screen effect. My primary guest and I on the right, our secondary guest on the left, whom the audience has only met in hyper-close-up until now.

Thousands of miles away the secondary guest settles onto their couch, anxiously eyeing their phone.

On the right rectangle of the screen, my primary guest and I nod to each other, on the left side the secondary guest gulps.

I punch in a number, while the secondary guest checks the time.

Within moments we are all connected. There are a few uncomfortable smiles, awkward stops and starts of overtalk, and confused grimaces as I settle us into the rhythm of this strange new dance.

Then, almost imperceptibly, the *Mission: Impossible* theme transitions into a softer, more melodic tune and the split-screen effect is replaced by alternating close-ups of my guests' faces.

Knowing chuckles replace uncomfortable gaps of silence. Smiles creep across cheeks. Attentive nods and soft *hmm*s say "we are listening."

"Wow," the secondary guest will say as our call nears its end, "I never thought of it that way."

"I now understand how your circumstances made you unaware of this problem which heretofore was not known to you," my primary guest will respond.

"I am deeply sorry for writing that offensive statement about you or to you," my secondary guest will offer.

"Apology fully accepted," my primary guest assures them.

"I . . . I am leaving this conversation changed," one declares.

"I, too, am leaving this conversation changed," the other responds.

"We are *all* leaving this conversation changed," I pipe up, nodding slowly, my voice breaking as a single tear rolls down my cheek.

Damn, I think, mindlessly shoveling metaphorical popcorn into my mouth as I watch this movie in my mind. *This is going to change the world.*

But as fun as this film is to watch, I know that I should actually start making it a reality.

◎

"Hey! I hope this message finds you well. You are doing The Work and we are all better for it," I type sycophantically in a Twitter DM to a celebrated writer. "I know your time is precious so I'll make this quick . . . I'm beginning to do preproduction on the second season where I will transition to the role of moderator and host a conversation between respected figures (like you) and a person who has written nasty stuff to/about you on the internet. Would love for you to be a guest." *Send*.

I write an almost identical message to an activist, and then a third to a popular comedian.

A blue circle finally appears on the top right-hand corner of Twitter's envelope icon. I click it and see that the writer has responded.

"I'm sorry Dylan. I admire what you're doing a great deal, but I am not prepared to have a conversation with these folk yet," he says.

Damn. I cross his name off my list. *One "no,"* I think.

Neither the activist nor the comedian respond, but I see that they both opened their messages immediately after I had sent them. I cross both of their names off my list, bringing us to a total of three no's.

A celebrated actor never responds. *Four*. Neither does the singer who has recently been clapping back at her haters publicly. *Five*. The local organizer who, only days earlier had proposed that we collaborate on a video, is silent. *Six*.

I wonder if instead of focusing on the guests first, I should instead let a compelling issue lead me to a primary guest rather than the other way around. #MeToo has just started trending on social media after two high-profile articles launch a public reckoning of sexual abuse in Hollywood. The hashtag has become a digital filing cabinet to which sexual assault and harassment survivors can bravely submit their own accounts, and thumb through the testimonies of others. I wonder how my project's new format might be able to speak to this powerful cultural moment and then I see that a journalist has come forward with her own account of workplace harassment. Delicately, I compose a message, in the hopes that she will find solace in connecting with a detractor who dismissed her account.

"Hey Dylan, this sounds interesting but I'm just becoming human again," she writes back. "Not sure if I should entertain anyone's negativity right now even if it's aimed at having a productive convo in the end. Appreciate you thinking of me and maybe we can revisit this down the line?" She punctuates this message with a red heart emoji.

"I totally understand," I reply. "Take all the time you need." *Seven.*

And then *eight* comes swiftly on its heels: "I realized I'm just not as brave as I thought," texts the chef who had been so excited by tl s idea a few weeks earlier.

As the rejections keep piling on, I don't understand why so many people seem so disinterested in something that has worked so well for me.

◎

2017 turns to 2018 and with the new year comes a fresh start that ends up just feeling like a continued losing streak. The athlete who had opened up to me about how online abuse affected her mental health asks that we delay any further production on her episode. *Nine.* An educator is uninterested in speaking to a man who publicly commented, "Who would want to have sex with her?" in response to her account of sexual assault. *Ten.*

I take these rejections in stride, though, because I have an amazing episode that has been quietly simmering in the background. One of my closest friends from childhood, who had originally expressed trepidation about this project, finally decided to take the plunge.

"Yeah i'd be down," he said, accepting my second invitation a few days ago.

A few mornings later, though, I wake up to a text.

"Hey love," he writes, "the more I think about it the more i think this isn't a good idea for me."

My eyes adjust to read the rest.

"Sorry to back out on you i just don't want to screw up what i have going this year." *Eleven.*

"I completely understand!" I say back. And I mean it, but this is the most disappointing one yet, so much so that I feel numb when a graphic artist backs out citing anxiety. *Twelve.*

Wondering if my approach is too focused on domestic matters, I get in touch with my Palestinian friend. As I type out the invitation, I foresee the power of hosting a discussion about an issue as enormous as the Israeli-Palestinian conflict, filtered through just two people, connecting across a historic divide. She writes back a few days later.

"Thanks so much for thinking of me for your podcast," her message begins.

Finally! I think. Then, I keep reading.

"To be honest," she continues, "the hate messages I get are more death threats than just hateful comments so I wouldn't want to engage with that or give them attention." *Thirteen.*

With so many rejections I wonder if I'm doing something wrong. Is it my wording? My approach? Do people just not like talking on the phone? I had gotten rejected before for this show. Many of my own detractors declined my invitation. Some had blocked me for even making the attempt. That made more sense to me, though. I, too, would be wary of coming onto a recorded phone call that would be hosted and edited by someone I had instructed to drown themselves. I understood that my skittish HATE FOLDER residents were simply protecting themselves. But what I don't get is why so few *recipients* of online hate are turning down this opportunity, too.

"I don't think I'm in a good enough mental health place to do the show," writes the designer whose episode I was already beginning to produce—*fourteen*—and the model who is finalizing her divorce says she can't do something "this emotionally challenging right now." *Fifteen.*

It has been months of trying to produce these moderated calls and I'm starting to get the sneaking suspicion that this new version of the project is unsustainable.

◎

After a couple days of respite, I take a closer look at this collection of rejections, which enables me to see something I hadn't before. Out of this pool of fifteen, the majority are Black, most are women, nearly half are queer, two are Arab, and one is trans. Which is to say that all of them occupy at least one marginalized identity. In my gut I know this isn't some strange coincidence.

I'm just becoming human again, said the journalist who came forward with a #MeToo allegation.

I just don't want to screw up what i have going this year, said my childhood friend, fearing a potential hate campaign against him.

The hate messages I get are more death threats, my Palestinian friend said.

All of them were trying to tell me that the vitriol they weathered was so bad that it had depleted them of any energy to have a conversation. And for those who didn't respond at all to my invitation, it was their silence that should have told me everything I needed to know: *Dylan, I don't have the energy to even* think *about this idea.*

But the correlation between my guests' marginalized identities and their lack of interest to speak to their detractors is anecdotal at best. Ten months from now, however, research will be published that corroborates this hunch with actual data.

In a study conducted by Amnesty International and Element AI that "surveyed millions of tweets received by 778 journalists and politicians from the UK and US throughout 2017," they will find that "7.1% of tweets sent to the women in the study were 'problematic' or 'abusive.'" Additionally, they will determine that "women of colour, (Black, Asian, Latinx, and mixed-race women) were 34% more likely to be mentioned in abusive or problematic tweets than white women." But most of all, "Black women were disproportionately targeted, being 84% more likely than white women to be mentioned in abusive or problematic tweets."

It makes total and depressing sense, then, that those who fight oppression every day in the physical world will then see that same bigotry mirrored in the digital sphere, too. And it also makes sense that those who receive the most online vitriol don't necessarily have a large reserve of energy to take part in an emotionally taxing conversation—no matter how well-intentioned it may be—when they are simply trying to survive. Just because *I* am excited to engage my detractors in conversation, clearly doesn't mean others are, too.

Looking back, I retroactively cringe at how brazenly I reached out to friends who were publicly sharing their pain, swooping in with an idea rather than support. I acted like some sort of digital ambulance chaser hoping to turn their online discontent into content, completely discounting the sheer energy it took to have these conversations, and the emotional cost of fostering radical empathy for adversarial internet strangers. This is particularly humbling to admit, as I have long regarded myself as well-versed in the intricacies and intersections of race and gender and sexuality. As a brown and queer person, I even *exist* at the intersection of marginalized identities. Still, in my own enthusiasm for this project—and the joy these conversations have given me—I had failed to see how understandably impossible this might be for others. Empathy across the divide is a luxury item that not everyone can afford.

The only comparison I can think to draw is that feeling you get at the pit of your stomach when someone far richer than you invites you out to a meal. You know the food will be decadent, the experience phenomenal, but you're terrified that at the end of the meal they'll request to split the bill, assuming that this amount of money means the same thing to you as it does to them. And if that gut-turning moment finally happens, you will furiously do the math in your head, determining whether or not your bank account can support your half, moving funds around in your brain all so that you can pay for your pasta and Diet Coke. In conversation, though, the bill is always split. And in this scenario, I was the rich person, nonchalant and unaware that this emotional bill was one that many couldn't afford—and shouldn't even have to pay in the first place.

◎

Of course, no group is a monolith. It would be a gross oversimplification to conclude that an entire demographic of people isn't interested in fostering radical empathy through conversation. And finally, due to either persistence, patience, or maybe just dumb luck, I am able to see that for myself.

In my first successful moderated phone call I connect Marcia and Andrew. Marcia is a stand-up comedian who has been repeatedly banned from Facebook for posting the words "men are scum" as a sort of performance art piece to highlight that the men who post "women are scum" don't get the same punishment. Andrew, who lives many states away, discovered Marcia's story through a popular antifeminist YouTuber. He called her a bigot in a comment. Their conversation is challenging, exhausting, and completely exhilarating. To even hear them on the phone with each other gives me the boost I need to keep going.

I host a call between two veterans of the Marines, Tyler and Maddie. In a since-deleted Facebook post, Tyler had supported the proposed ban that would prohibit transgender soldiers from serving in the military. Maddie, who had recently come out as trans herself, is against the ban. Their conversation flows beautifully as they share literal war stories with each other, and while thanking Maddie at the end of their call, Tyler reveals that she is the first transgender Marine he's ever met. This conversation is everything I dreamed that this format would allow.

When I connect Jaya and Tom, I don't know what to expect. Jaya is a journalist who had recently written an article for *GQ* that questioned how the beloved sitcom *The Office* holds up in an era when we as a culture are coming to terms with the reality of toxic workplace behavior. In response, a stranger named Tom wrote that Jaya "should be burned at the stake for disrespecting the office." But I listen closely as they ease into their conversation and savor the moment when they discover their surprising overlap with the sitcom that brought them together in the first place: For both, it was a show that they shared with a parent—Tom with his mom, and Jaya with her dad. Throughout the call, they both listen to each other, laughing along the way, and by the end of it we are all making loose plans to grab sushi together.

◎

I believe in conversation. And how could I not? I see how well it works, especially as a sort of breakout room from the dehumanizing game of the internet that only allows us to see each other from across a canyon. These phone calls make that canyon a little smaller, even if only for a moment, by allowing us to see each other more fully.

Tyler had never met a trans marine before Maddie and now he

can say that he has. Tom got to hear Jaya narrate the subtle terrors of workplace misogyny. Andrew and Marcia became closer, even if only for an hour, simply by speaking to each other rather than communicating in the warped funhouse mirror of social media.

These moments I get to witness on these calls make me so overwhelmed with joy and possibility that I feel so unspeakably lucky to even witness them. These are the moments when I feel less like a host and more like a person who somehow wrangled their way into a front row seat at a once-in-a-lifetime show.

But believing in something for yourself does not mean that we should then demand that everyone else experience it, too. I still think that conversation is a form of activism, but I also believe that activism is a mosaic, and that, like a mosaic, there are many tiles which all work together to tell a bigger story. There are many ways to move forward, many forms of activism, many tiles. Conversation is just one of them.

I recall the conservative listener who applauded me for doing this project. "I have never found anyone, I mean anyone, that has your points of view and could have a calm and respectful conversation," he said. When I first read this, I felt like some bold unicorn doing what others *should* be doing but weren't brave enough to do. But now that I understand why more people don't want to do this, this praise feels like a gift I must regretfully decline. To accept it without qualification would be to discount the potential guests who very understandably don't have the emotional resources to practice the art of "calm and respectful conversation."

Bravery, it turns out, is not one thing. There are many ways to be brave. It's brave to have difficult conversations with someone who hurt you online. I also think it's brave to protect yourself and know your limits well enough to articulate when you *don't* want to have a conversation.

If fostering empathy is a luxury, then the virtue that is projected on me for having these conversations feels like a rich person being praised for their beautiful home. Sure, that kitchen remodel is stunning, and yes that parquet flooring is the pinnacle of elegance, but it's not hard to have good taste when you have the resources to procure it. It's easy to foster radical empathy for your detractors when it's something you feel well suited to do.

So, I trudge forward, thrilled for all of the phone calls that lay ahead, ready to keep making connections with my guests, while newly conscious of the many who will not be able to afford this project's pricey entrance fee.

8

interrogation is not conversation

"Dylan?" a woman asks hesitantly as she approaches me.

"Yes!" I exclaim perhaps too emphatically as I stand to greet her. "And you're . . . Emma, right?" I mimic her same uncertain tone, pretending that I don't know exactly who she is.

Like anyone who even passively pays attention to cultural news, I know Emma Sulkowicz's story. Or, to be fair, I know what I've heard of her story. I know, for example, that in 2014 she became the face of campus sexual assault survivors when she began carrying a mattress around her university's campus as a form of symbolic protest. I know that her story was picked up by every major news outlet and that because of her ubiquity in public consciousness she was dubbed "mattress girl." I know that every time I passed the campus around 2014, I would always crane my neck to see if I could catch a glimpse of this heroic piece of history in the making. And I also know that tonight we are about to have dinner.

The person standing before me looks different from the Emma I knew from pictures. She is four years older now, no longer a college student. In place of the shoulder-length hair I had come to recognize, this Emma has short blue hair.

"Is this okay?" I ask, gesturing to the table I've been holding for us by the window.

"It's great!" she exclaims with a hearty laugh.

There is no set agenda for this meal; we're simply two people who want to get to know each other. A few weeks earlier we'd been connected through email by her dad, Kerry, whom I had met at a conference. As the evening progresses, I feel like I'm catching up with an old friend. Emma has an infectious laugh that bubbles up from within her before it explodes into a smile. She's excited to talk about her art, and she is, I'm coming to see, ferociously smart.

When we transition to talking about my work, I tell her about *Conversations with People Who Hate Me*, its origins, and its evolution into the moderated format. Her eyes widen with fascination; I see that she understands it in a way that many don't. Emma is an artist and seems to fully appreciate my project's foundation as a social experiment–performance art hybrid. She then opens up about her own experience with online hate—a tsunami compared to what I've been through.

"Would you ever be interested in doing an episode?" I blurt out, perhaps preemptively.

"Oh!" she says, in shock that that was even a possibility. "Can I think about it?"

"Of course!" I say, but I'm sure that her answer will be *no*. And when that happens, I will completely understand. Rape survivors, especially public rape survivors, receive an onslaught of digital abuse simply for coming forward. *Empathy is a luxury*, I remind myself.

I leave the dinner hoping that we'll see each other again, but sure it won't be for this show. So, I'm particularly surprised when I find an email in my inbox from Emma a week later in which she writes: "Let's make an episode together!"

Throughout the following weeks, Emma and I exchange a flurry of emails, texts, and phone calls as we hatch a plan to find a secondary guest who is, according to the phrase I've now rehearsed dozens of times, "Negative enough to merit inclusion, but not so hateful as to feel unsafe."

"We have so many options now!" Emma writes in an email's subject line.

When I click to open it, my eyes widen as I see ten screenshots. Ten mystery boxes, each containing a vicious surprise.

"Disgusting pig," reads one.

"You're a dumb stupid excuse for a female," reads another. "A true whore."

"You are a lier," reads a third, with a typo softening the message's accusation.

Beside each screenshot is a link to the author's profile. One by one I click these links, which immediately transport me to the digital doorsteps of Emma's detractors. Some of these men have hidden themselves behind impenetrable fortresses of a locked profile with little available information save for an alma mater and a low-resolution profile picture. Others seem like the distant villains you might expect to send these messages—users whose recent posts might include a misogynistic meme or a xenophobic rant. Others, however, look like they could be old college friends of mine with the kind, neutral faces that disappear into the infinite galaxy of social media acquaintances. It's easy to get lost in this step of the process, to fall into the rabbit hole of a stranger's hypothetical life, so I remind myself that I'm only here to figure out two things. One: *Does this person feel safe?* And two: *Will this message yield an interesting conversation?*

The anonymous senders seem too unknown and the misogynistic meme lords feel too scary, so I click on the profile of the person who called Emma a "lier." I meet a man smiling at the camera beside two women who look like family members. Who are they? *Focus, Dylan.* Who is he? His name, I learn, is Jonathan. And, to answer my first question, yes. He does feel safe. And now, to the second.

When rape survivors come forward with an allegation, they often face a chorus of doubters who press with endless questions and comments about the legitimacy of their claims even though studies have shown that false allegations are incredibly rare. A 2010 study, for example, found that only between 2 percent and 10 percent of reported allegations are false. This number ostensibly gets even lower when considering the Department of Justice's finding in 2002 that 63 percent of rapes aren't even reported in the first place. But even *this* number doesn't tell the whole story because it doesn't account for male rape victims. On top of an actual trial—if they even reach that step—high-profile cases are often given a perpetual hearing in the Court of Public Opinion, that intangible space that exists in the collective consciousness just off of the public square, where denizens can serve as jurors, prosecutors, audience members, and judges all at once.

As I look at Jonathan's four-word message I muse about how their conversation might go. I like to visualize all of my phone calls as existing in a room somewhere in the cloud of digital telephone wires—an intimate dance floor floating in a void where my guests' voices circle each other, before retreating back to their separate lives. This room, this suspended dance floor, is a respite from the game of social media, a shelter from the Everything Storm, and it sits on the opposite side of town from the Debate Arena. Best of all, this room is nowhere near the Court of Public Opinion. How, I wonder, will Emma and Jonathan interact in this room?

"What do you think about Jonathan?" I ask Emma a few days later, my phone jammed between my shoulder and my ear as I browse his profile again.

"Jonathan . . ." she repeats blankly, trying to place him. "Wait, which one is he? I can't keep them straight!" She breaks out into a laugh at the absurdity of how many options there are. In the background I hear her open her laptop to consult the archive she had sent. "Oh! Jonathan! He's not even the worst one."

"I know, but I think he's our guy." I say confidently enough. "How do you feel about it?"

"If you're down, I'm down!"

"Hello?" a voice answers.

Not long ago this voice was just a screenshot and a link. Now it's attached to a full human being.

"Jonathan?" I ask.

"Hi."

For each moderated episode, I make sure to interview the primary and secondary guests separately before their group call. This eases both of them into an understandably daunting experience, but it's especially important for the secondary guest. Unlike Emma, Jonathan and I have not eaten dinner together, we have not been giddily talking about this episode on the phone, and we have not opened up to each other about why we make the work we make. I recognize that he might feel outnumbered and skeptical. It takes guts to own up to something you've written online so I use these solo calls to signal to my secondary guest *Hey, you can trust me.*

"This is not a shaming podcast," I clarify at the beginning of our call. "There's no villain, there's no victim."

Many secondary guests get skittish at this point, terrified that I'm actually their employer who has gone undercover to extract a confession before I fire them. I need to make it clear that he's not in trouble, that I am not the authorities, and, most important, that he is not being put on trial for what he has written to Emma. Now that I feel like I've earned his trust, I can move on to my favorite part: getting to know him.

Jonathan tells me that he is twenty-four years old, and is nearly finished with college, save for a few outstanding credits, but has been making some money trading stocks and hasn't wanted to go back since. As he speaks, I can hear the faint hint of an accent but maybe I'm projecting it onto him because I can see his hometown on Facebook. He sounds sweet and gentle. Polite, well-mannered. He hasn't dated in a while, and confesses that it can get lonely, but overall he's "certainly very blessed." He is, he tells me, a straight white man.

"Hopefully that doesn't marginalize me to a certain demographic of your audience," he jokes.

"No," I assure him, "we accept all types here."

He tells me that he wrote that message to Emma because, "based on the evidence, it was just hard to believe her claims were as she was representing them." He doesn't remember the exact outlets but can vaguely recall that he was getting his information from "multiple articles, multiple sources." Emma's accusation hit him particularly hard because he was a senior in high school at the time, "on the cusp of college," and hoping for a relationship himself. The fear of being labeled a rapist, he tells me, is "a really serious thing for a person's life."

"Are there any specific questions you have for Emma?" I ask him, trying to foment his curiosity for tomorrow's group call.

"I mean, right now, no. I don't want to . . . Because I have empathy for her, too, now. After all this dust has settled, I'm sure this has been . . . God only knows the kind of things that people have said to her," he responds. "I'm totally willing to have my mind changed."

"I think that's the healthiest approach to take for life," I tell him, grateful for his elasticity.

I'm hopeful that through the simple act of talking to Emma, hearing her voice, and getting to know her, Jonathan will realize that the person he's talking to, the person whose claims he once doubted, is real and not just a distant name in a news story.

"This podcast is based on asking questions," I tell him, almost as homework for tomorrow's recording. Questions, as I discovered on my call with E, are one of the strongest ways to resist the Debate Arena.

"Well," I say, wrapping up the call, "the next step is that you and Emma will talk to each other."

"Awesome," he says. "I look forward to it."

"All right. How are you feeling?"

"I'm so excited," Emma shoots back, fully amped up.

We are sitting at my dining room table, facing each other through a forest of microphone arms, XLR cables, and headphone wires. It's an unseasonably hot Wednesday afternoon in late May, and Emma and I are soaking up the last gusts of Freon before we have to turn off the air conditioner for recording purposes. After a month of coordinating, we are finally here.

I dial Jonathan's number.

"Hello?" Jonathan answers immediately, his voice suddenly appearing in both of our headphones.

"Hey, Jonathan!" I exclaim out of true delight. "Emma, this is Jonathan. Jonathan, this is Emma."

"Hi, Jonathan. I just want to say that I'm so excited that you're doing this, and I'm so excited that this is happening. Thank you."

"Likewise," he replies cordially. "Thank *you.*"

A surge of excitement courses through me. Construction has begun on that ephemeral room.

"Jonathan, a few years ago, you wrote Emma a message with very few words. You just said, 'You are a lier.'" I find it best to rip off the Band-Aid early. "Emma, how did it feel to receive it?"

"Honestly, it wasn't even just Jonathan's message individually that hurt so much. It was the torrential outpouring from the internet of these kinds of messages into my lap."

Emma is instinctively doing something I have found to be successful on my own phone calls. By separating Jonathan, the individual, from the entirety of the hate she received, she's assuring him that he is not the sole villain. Emma is providing what I can only think to call an empathy cushion—a soft pad of understanding that allows the conversation to move forward.

"I apologize for the hurt," Jonathan declares. "I do sincerely apologize for that."

I hadn't expected a direct apology this soon, but it feels amazing. And just as I'm reveling in the glory of this moment, Jonathan continues his sentence.

"But," he says. "I don't apologize for the disagreement."

Maybe it was unrealistically hopeful of me to think that reconciliation would happen right away.

"You became a very public person, right?" Jonathan presses on. "Maybe some messages should be expected."

Jonathan is being a little more forthright than I thought he'd be, but I assume this is the usual defensiveness that rears its head in the early moments of these calls.

"I think it's really important that I just kind of repeat the story as it went down," Emma says, offering to walk Jonathan through everything that happened after her assault. I watch as she steels herself, harnessing all the energy she can to revisit this time in her life, but I trust that it will be worth it. By hearing the story from Emma herself, his skepticism of her claims will surely dissolve.

"I just wanted it to go away," she recalls wishing right after her assault. She only came to terms with what happened after learning that it wasn't just her—her accused assailant seemed to have left a trail of other victims. Eventually, she and two of the other women who accused him of assault reported him to the campus's rape crisis center, but the accused student managed to postpone the case for almost a year. Simultaneously, a student journalist was writing an article for the university's magazine and interviewed Emma along with her fellow survivors for a piece that explored how the university handled rape cases. Though all of the survivors remained anonymous, the story quickly blew up on campus.

While this was happening, Senator Kirsten Gillibrand was drafting a bill to reform how college rape cases are handled and one of her aides reached out to the student journalist to see if any of the survivors wanted to go public. Emma was the only one to volunteer. "I was just like, 'Shit, if no one else is going to do it, then I guess I have to do it,'" she recounts to Jonathan. And there she found herself, speaking to the nation's press, retelling her story. People immediately criticized her for not going to the police, and as a self-identified rule follower, she took the advice of her new critics and called law enforcement at the end of her junior year. But when they came to question her she recalls how cruel they were, how they suggested it wasn't rape because she and her accused assailant had had consensual sex before, how they dismissed her claims of his violent abuse as "weird," and how one detective she met with labeled her accused rapist's actions as "creative" rather than "violent." The case, Emma explains, was then transferred from person to person, forcing her to retell the story over and over again until finally it reached the district attorney who told her that the case might take a year to go to trial. This meant that she would already have graduated. "I had to call the whole thing off," she tells Jonathan. "It's more of an emotional toll on me than it is productive." Instead, she figured, she would just go make art at the residency that she had been invited to attend that summer.

"Jonathan, can I even tell you how I came up with Mattress Performance?" she asks, pausing her story to check in with him.

"Sure!" he exclaims gamely.

Emma bursts with a laugh. "I hope I'm not completely boring you," she says with a huge smile on her face.

"No," Jonathan politely replies, "the information I have is from just articles and the internet, so it's good to hear right from the source."

We have made it to the room. The dance floor is being polished.

With Jonathan's blessing, Emma continues, telling him how, at this artist residency she had the freedom to do anything she wanted. To document her artistic process, she asked a friend to film her as she cleared furniture out of a room and when she reviewed the footage, she became transfixed by an unintentional, throwaway moment: her moving a mattress, how she struggled underneath the weight of it, but carried it anyway.

Inspired by this observation and the performance artist Tehching Hsieh, whose physically taxing pieces were performed over long periods of time, Emma had the idea to carry a mattress around her campus for the entirety of her senior year in a site-specific performance art piece that she would call "Mattress Performance." She didn't think it would become a big deal and was sure that she would just recede into the background, quietly hauling around this unwieldy piece of furniture until graduation. But by the end of her first day reporters followed her out of her dorm room, and suddenly it turned into something very different than what she had imagined. The media moniker of "mattress girl" was coined and she was unceremoniously thrust back into the national spotlight.

"So anyway, Jonathan," Emma concludes, "I say this all to just, I mean, I hope give you a clearer picture of how people will say things like, 'Oh, but you put yourself in the public eye,' and it's kind of by accident. I wonder how you take that."

"Well, first of all, thank you for telling me all that," Jonathan replies. "I've never had anything go viral. Intuitively I could see how things just explode. And you were a college student. And not knowing exactly how to handle that. I mean, all I can do is just put myself in your shoes as best I can."

Great! I think, *Jonathan is starting to come around! I can hear the seeds of understanding sprouting within him. Now we can move onto—*

"But I mean," he pivots, "you did continue to carry the mattress. I guess, I don't really know what to say. And you were on the cover of the magazine . . ."

I'm starting to notice a strange pattern. It seems like every time Jonathan takes a step forward with empathy, he frequently follows it up by retreating back. Like some sort of conversational riptide. An offer, then a withdrawal. An offer, a withdrawal.

"Thank you for saying that," Emma says genuinely, "and I very much understand that the media wants you to feel inflamed about me, because the media makes money when people are, like, totally freaking out, you know?"

Emma is offering Jonathan another empathy cushion. Perhaps this is the remedy for the riptide.

"I think rape is completely abhorrent, and I promise you I'm one hundred percent with you, you just have to believe me. You have to trust me on that," Jonathan states. "But—"

There it is again: the withdrawal of a kind offer.

"But I would encourage any listeners or viewers to go and read about it. The actual events, as they were reported, the texts that were released."

"Wait. The texts that were released by whom?" I ask, truly unsure of what he's talking about.

"The texts that were released in the case," Jonathan replies.

I suddenly remember that he had brought these up in our solo interview, but I hadn't known what he was talking about. I defer to Emma to see if she's comfortable exploring this, which, she says, she is.

The texts, I learn, are a series of Facebook messages between Emma and her accused assailant that this man transcribed and released as part of a lawsuit he filed against the university in retaliation. Jonathan seems to be reading these transcribed texts from an article and, after a few minutes of messily setting up my computer for her, Emma pulls up the messages herself. Delicately, she reads each one aloud to him, and identifies where the texts had been intentionally cut off—whether by her accused assailant, the journalist who published the texts, or both—and how that changes their meaning. She explains some inside jokes she had with her friends at the time and how, in context, they don't look so jarring. Jonathan confirms he can now see that they're cut off.

"I guess I'm curious, Jonathan," Emma gently begins, "if now that I've filled in a bit of that stuff, do you still feel like the evidence stacks up against me?"

"I'm definitely more inclined than I was an hour ago to believe what you're saying as the absolute truth. I just wish somehow I could have all the information right in front of me, you know?"

Throughout the next hour Jonathan's riptides keep coming. He mostly believes women, *but* he thinks that men are also wrongfully accused. He feels empathy for women who have been raped, *but* he says it's nuanced. He feels bad for the harassment Emma has received from "douchebags," *but* he still has questions. He finds Emma more believable, *but* he still thinks listeners should do their own research. He understands that Emma was thrust into the public eye, *but* he doesn't fully understand why she kept carrying the mattress. He sees how Emma is a role model, *but* has different opinions on her case.

"I'm in a weird ambiguous place," he says, "I'm just saying it's hard for me to take the evidence and call somebody a rapist from what I've seen. But I'm not saying it didn't happen, either."

"I was hoping and feeling that we'd talked about a lot of the details in the case that were confusing to you," Emma says. I hear a hint of frustration in her voice. "Is there stuff that you're still unclear on?"

Jonathan takes this as an invitation to seek out the answers he feels he's missing. He doesn't understand the timeline of events, he is confused by the fact that Emma made a video in which she re-created her assault, and he wants clarity as to why Emma turned it into an art project for a school credit. "So, is it, just, like . . . Is it all art?" he asks, exasperated in his seemingly fruitless quest for clarity.

Emma diligently answers all of these questions one by one. "When I'm sad or upset or angry, I just make an artwork about it," she explains.

"And then you also did, like, a bondage thing?" The questions don't seem to stop.

Something is feeling different about this conversation, I just can't quite put my finger on what that is. I need to get us back on track, but I can't find the solution to a problem I have yet to diagnose. We are not in the game of social media; we are on an intimate phone call. The Everything Storm is nowhere on the horizon; on the contrary, we have been hyperfocused on one single topic. This doesn't feel like a debate, either. So, what is happening? Is it the conversational riptides? I think those are more of a symptom of the problem than the cause. I glance at the timecode on my recorder. Exhaustion is rising in their voices. Emma is feeling grilled, and Jonathan isn't getting the answers he's looking for. Begrudgingly I decide that this feels like a good enough ending point.

"So, guys, we're coming to the close of the call," I say wearily. "I just want to check in: Jonathan, how are you feeling about the call?"

"It was great. I really appreciate the opportunity. It's been a real pleasure," he says cheerily.

Then, I look to Emma.

"I started out feeling really excited and feeling like 'oh great, I can explain what happened to this guy, and then he'll understand,'" she says, trying to talk through her fatigue. "But last time we checked in I felt like you still didn't really feel like you could believe me. And so, I guess I feel a little like my wings have been clipped. And I'm a little sad and crushed." She laughs to punctuate this but it's different from her buoyant laugh. This one is offset by the disappointment I see in her face.

"It's not that I don't believe you," Jonathan tries to assure her. "It's just so hard to prove just definitively, and that's sort of what I need before I ruin a person's reputation. Because that's how I'd want to be treated, you know?"

In any other conversation, this revelation—his admission that his resistance to believe her is rooted in a fear of how *he* might be treated—would have been a beautiful moment of introspection that could have unlocked so many beautiful new avenues of exploration. This could have evolved into a nuanced discussion about American masculinity, and how some truly good men have been terrified that a false allegation may come for all of them one day. But now I fear that that ship has sailed. Emma has been so busy defending herself that I see her energy draining fast.

"I think one thing that would be good to clarify," Emma begins, "is that you were, like, 'Look, I don't ever want to ruin someone's life and falsely accuse them of rape.' Right? That's something you don't want to do?"

"Right," Jonathan says.

"That is also something that *I* never want to do. I would feel sick if I falsely accused someone of rape. I think that would be a step backwards for the feminist movement." Emma is delivering this calmly, but directly. "Given that, I accused someone of rape. So, I think a big part of it is that you would have to trust me to be the kind of person who would never want to falsely accuse someone of rape. And the only reason I would ever accuse someone of rape is if they did it. Does that kind of logically make sense?"

Surely this will be the thing that finally reaches Jonathan. The ultimate point that allows him to believe her.

"It makes sense logically, but I just can't—I can't do that. I don't do that with anybody. You sound like a very nice person. I'm not calling that into question, but I don't—that isn't enough for me to believe somebody is a rapist. I need proof. I need it beyond a shadow of a doubt. That's what I need. Forensic . . . video . . . It's just what I need."

This recommitment to his doubt thrusts us back into another impasse, another tangent—yet another detour into yet another topic.

This time it's the fallibility of forensic evidence, the inability of rape kits to detect revoked consent, and the way some police departments mishandle rape accusations.

"It's unimaginable to me that that would happen," Jonathan says of police officers disrespecting a rape survivor. "I can't imagine it."

Only now can I see the profound difference in how they each see the world. Jonathan is not advocating on behalf of a vicious world, but the world that ought to be. The world where good prevails and evil is destroyed when we follow the rules. The world he *thinks* we live in. But Emma is speaking from the world that *is*, the world she has seen up close, the world that she has found a way to survive out of necessity.

"Did you, when you sent that message, have any idea that I might be receiving hundreds just like it?" she asks him. This is the first time in the call that she isn't offering him an empathy cushion, and is instead directly addressing the hurt that he caused her.

"No," Jonathan replies directly. "That's true. I did not put myself in your shoes and say, 'this is probably . . . this could just be more BS,' like 'somebody else has already said this.' 'It doesn't need to be said.' Yeah, I didn't think about that."

Perhaps this is as close as we're going to get to resolution. *This is it? This is the end of the call? What happened?*

"I'm sorry for ever sending the message," Jonathan says, "and I'm sorry I hurt your feelings. I am sorry about that."

"Well, thank you for that. I feel like we've taken this as far as it can go," Emma says flatly.

I look at her across the table, through the forest of headphone wires and microphone cables, the same view I had at the beginning of the call when she was brimming with excitement, but now she looks deflated and drained.

Most goodbyes on the show have been somewhere between pleasant and deeply cathartic. A few pairs of guests in moderated episodes have asked to be put in touch, some maintain thriving digital friendships, while the majority, at least, walk away with a quiet gratitude for the experience. But not today. Today feels different.

"Are there any final things you want to say to each other? Parting words?" I ask.

Jonathan goes first. "I appreciate this opportunity a lot. This is . . . I would have never imagined that sending that message would allow me to actually speak to the person. And I know it may be hard to believe me, Emma, and the viewers or whatever, but I really wish this person, Emma, all the best in life, only the good things for you. May you have a long life and a great life. And you as well, Dylan. And again, I appreciate the opportunity."

"Thank you, Jonathan," Emma says, genuinely but dejected.

"Emma? Any final words?"

"Yeah, this has been, you know . . . it's definitely really retraumatizing to have to talk about all this stuff because this is the kind of stuff I had to tell the school hearing committee. This is the kind of stuff I had to tell the police officers. This is the kind of stuff I had to tell so many people who wouldn't believe me, and it's kind of just . . . it breaks my heart to do it again and to feel like the person on the other side can't believe me because I can't provide them with this science that they needed. So, yeah, I'm definitely going away from this conversation feeling like a little . . . like I'll never have the kind of resolution I've wanted. And, you know, it's always sad because it's, like, I never wanted to be raped in the first place. I never wanted to be here at all. So, yeah, I'm coming away from this conversation a little heartbroken and I guess . . . I hope that this conversation ends up meaning something to someone someday."

This devastating end to what I was sure was going to be a profound episode has now become a profound disappointment. Looking at Emma completely exhausted allows me to finally understand that this wasn't a conversation at all. This was an interrogation. We aren't in the poetic room in the cloud of digital telephone wires—we never were. This is the Court of Public Opinion and Emma was on trial.

This podcast is based on asking questions, I remember telling Jonathan on our solo call to stoke his curiosity. By encouraging him to ask whatever questions he wanted, I had helped incite an investigation. His doubt had calcified into a crusade for answers, and by inviting him to the conversation I had given him license to continue on this quest. All this time I had been so concerned with ensuring that Jonathan didn't feel the sting of accusation for what he had written, that I had failed to realize that Emma would be thrust into the role of defendant by default for what she had lived.

◉

"Jon is a simpleton and the stereotypical privileged male," writes one person on Facebook.

"That guy Jonathan was almost psychopathic," writes another.

"Jon, if you're reading this, I hope you're eaten alive by wild dogs," a third commenter says.

"You dumbshit asshole, and your inability to form a logical thought can fuck right off. Fuck you."

The comment section beneath my post about Jonathan and Emma's episode reads like an anti-Jonathan meet-up. Their conversation has been released only hours ago, and it already seems to be eliciting a strong response. For a while I wasn't even sure that I was going to release it, but with Emma's blessing I forged ahead with the editing and postproduction process. Now it's finally out in the world.

As I read through these comments, it strikes me as sadly ironic that Jonathan is getting a tiny taste of what it feels like to exist publicly, his own mini hearing in the Court of Public Opinion. But this worries me, too. If my goal is to open Jonathan's mind, I'm concerned that this onslaught of negativity will make him double down. No matter how much I may understand the anger from so many listeners in the comment section, this doesn't feel like justice. Jonathan, like all my previous guests, did not create this culture of disbelieving rape survivors. He simply upheld it unknowingly.

This experience was challenging for everyone—for Emma, for the listeners, for Jonathan, and for me. And since I can't undo it, the next best thing I can do is learn from it.

Curiosity is not inherently virtuous. Simply asking questions does not automatically lead to a productive conversation. In fact, it can be a recipe for disaster. If conversation is an improvised dance, where each participant feels like they're getting and giving in equal parts, then interrogation is a ceaseless drilling, an emotionally reckless deep dive for answers no matter the cost.

Going into this call, I had been so sure that my main job was to get Emma and Jonathan on the phone with each other. And if I steered them clear of the Everything Storm and made sure we didn't enter the Debate Arena, that just by hearing each other's voices and listening to each other's stories, that things would just kind of sort themselves out. That an empathic connection would kind of, like, *happen*. I didn't know that we could be served a surprise summons to the Court of Public Opinion, and that I wouldn't realize where we were until closing arguments had wrapped.

With public figures, it can be especially easy to feel that we are owed an explanation. Our minds often flatten them into symbols of what we want them to be, transforming them into projection screens onto which we transpose our dreams and fantasies and biases and preconceived notions and the cultural narratives we have unknowingly inherited. And so, when given an opportunity to talk to them, we feel that we are owed something. So, we dig and we dig and we dig, forgetting that they are human, too.

But this isn't just about public figures. Any conversation can fall prey to the gravitational pull of the interrogation room, the clumsy default into the witness box. Many of us feel that we are owed something from those who are different, people who live in a way we *just don't get*. People whose stories *don't make sense*. People who our friends teach us to joke about. And sometimes we mistakenly think our curiosity entitles us to answers, forgetting that curiosity—that noble seed—can quickly devolve into a brutal cross-examination. So, we drill for answers, forgetting that we're talking to a human being who will understandably tire the more we drill.

Ultimately, interrogation is the antagonist of conversation because it dehumanizes everyone involved. The person being interrogated feels like an object, ceaselessly plumbed for information. And they suddenly have to be on the defense, a tough position from which to engender empathy. But it also dehumanizes the interrogator, too. It changes their goal from exploration to extraction, gradually transforming them from a human being into an oil rig, pumping and pumping for answers that they'll never get. And in the end no one is seen, no one is seeing, and instead everyone feels like they didn't get justice in a space where they thought they might.

This call has been my most challenging yet, and for a moment I question whether or not it's right to continue this project. *Maybe it's run its course*, I think.

But then I start to see messages come in. Notes from rape survivors who listened and recognized themselves in the conversation.

"Hearing Emma and how she so perfectly addressed Jonathan's concerns was in itself, healing," writes a man who opened up to me about his own sexual assault.

"This conversation hit me hard because I can relate to so much of what you are saying," another person writes in an email to Emma and me. "I just really wanted to thank you for being brave and being a voice for us."

"Hearing this hasn't so much triggered me as it has caused me to reflect on what would have happened if I had called the cops," writes a man whose rapist forced him into silence.

These listeners make me proud to have released this difficult episode. Seeing how many of them saw themselves in Emma is a sobering reminder of this issue's relevance. But I'm particularly surprised to see that some see their reflection in Jonathan, too.

"It was extremely brave for her to do what she did and nothing short of real-life heroism," writes a first-time listener. "I believe her and feel a great deal of shame that I ever doubted her. It changed my mind and frankly if you ask me I think it changed the caller's mind also, it may just be hard for him to admit it while recording. MAYBE check back in a week or two after the conversation stews with him."

9

the makeover illusion

Home improvement shows. People keep asking how I unwind after hosting these conversations and that is my honest answer: home improvement shows. Specifically, *Fixer Upper.*

The premise of *Fixer Upper* is simple. "We take the worst house in the best neighborhood, and we turn it into our clients' dream home," the show's tagline proclaims. The "we" is husband-and-wife team Chip and Joanna Gaines—Jo, affectionately—and every episode follows the exact same structure: In the show's first act, Chip and Jo meet a Texan couple in search of a home. Together they show the couple three houses that can be placed somewhere on the scale between "slightly outdated" and "legally condemned." The couple then selects one of the three options, at which point our beloved hosts divide and conquer. Jo walks the couple through a fancy digital rendering of their proposed renovation, while Chip and a crew of mostly unnamed laborers begin demolishing the old walls and furnishings. "Demo day!" Chip says, delighted, into the camera almost every time this stage is reached. We then watch along as new walls are built, shiplap is installed, and kitchen backsplashes are artfully arranged with Jo's discerning eye. Chip will usually find a problem in the show's third act—faulty wiring, an improperly installed drainpipe, a leaky roof—and invariably that problem is fixed in the episode's fourth act thanks to his quick thinking and deft hand. Once Chip's work is done, Jo will spend the final few nights before the Big Reveal tirelessly staging the home with artfully appointed furniture and, every so often, a family heirloom that she has encased in glass. Finally, about six minutes before the end of the episode, the new homeowners are gathered before a life-sized picture of their old house, which Chip and Jo pull apart to reveal their newly refurbished home. The homeowners will jump up and down, cry, and scream, and then they'll walk through the open space where a wall used to be and say *Wow* and *You really outdid yourself this time* and *You are making a grown man cry* and *It exceeds our wildest dreams.*

I love *Fixer Upper* because it's the opposite of *Conversations with People Who Hate Me.* While Chip and Jo can confidently guarantee a radical transformation at the end of each episode, the only thing I can offer is the quiet peace that is reached when two strangers have listened to each other with the tacit understanding that everyone will go back to their lives once we hang up. And while the structure of each *Fixer Upper* episode is essentially the same, every phone call I record feels like a new obstacle course whose takeaways I'm scrambling to absorb even after the call has ended. I wish my phone calls could offer the same dramatic satisfaction as a forty-three-minute episode of *Fixer Upper.* And, in a strange way, I watch their show with a bit of envy, wondering how I might be able to pull off such a satisfying conclusion.

It is September of 2018 and I'm nearing the end of my project's second season. I need a break. I've been working on *Conversations with People Who Hate Me* for nearly a year and a half straight. At this point I've reached out to more than two hundred and fifty prospective guests, recorded almost thirty phone calls, and have released twenty-two of those recordings as episodes.

For the most part, these conversations have been going quite well.

I recently hosted a call between two friends who had unfriended each other on Facebook over their disagreement regarding which Democratic candidate to support in a primary election and, after we hung up, I learned that they had re-friended each other online. I also connected two Latin American strangers who disagreed about the value of the gender-neutral term *latinx* and that turned into a lovely exploration of culture and how we react when we fear that it's being taken away from us. And whenever I speak to my own detractors we often disagree while still acknowledging each other's humanity. Most calls have been dances, and any conversation that avoids the Everything Storm, resists the pull of the Debate Arena, and steers clear of the interrogation booth counts as a success to me. But no matter how great these calls feel, there's something I still can't get out of my head.

After the first season of the podcast an acquaintance wrote me an email. "Dude, I've listened to every ep of your podcast, and it is fascinating and well made but FUCKING INFURIATING," his email began. "Who is your intended audience for the show? I ask because I listen to your podcast, and all I do is go 'omg Dylan is a saint' and 'UGH, FUCK THESE FUCKING STUPID BIGOTS'. So, I'm starting to get the feeling your intended audience is not me. Which is totally fine! I just started to think, what is the point of this?"

By now I can nearly recite his email verbatim as I think about it quite often. For one thing, I bristle at his diagnosis of my guests. While I do profoundly disagree with certain beliefs that some of my guests hold, now that I've spoken to them, I see them as full human beings and can't write them off as one thing. Plus, by accepting my invitation to talk they've taken accountability for what they've written, which is more than most can say. But what gets me most about this email is his last question: *What is the point of this?* This question still crawls under my skin just as much today as it did when I received it a year ago. I resent it, not because it's unfair, but because it makes me jealous of Chip and Jo. No one would ever dare ask them to define the point of *their* show. They take the worst houses in the best neighborhoods and turn it into their client's dream home. So how can I show him the point of my project? How can I capture a transformation in one of my recordings?

As I consider different ways to close out the show's second season, I keep thinking about one conversation that didn't have the resolution that I had dreamed of. A conversation that has become a thorn in my side. A conversation that is the equivalent of a *Fixer Upper* episode ending the moment Chip finds a faulty electric box.

I have an idea. But first, I need to make a few calls.

◎

The phone rings. I have no idea what to expect. It rings again. *Is he gonna pick up?*

"Dylan?" the voice answers. It's a familiar voice, but one I haven't heard in a while.

"Hey, Jonathan. How are you?"

It's been over three months since we've spoken. The last words we exchanged voice-to-voice were our goodbyes at the end of his particularly tough conversation with Emma, and in the months since I've been trying to figure out what I could have done differently.

"What was that experience like for you to be on the podcast?" I ask him.

"Retrospectively, I wish I'd been a little bit more thoughtful," Jonathan says. "I was kind of entrenched at the time and more defensive than I should have been." He sounds far more relaxed, more reflective than he had been on his call with Emma.

Jonathan then tells me that he had read some of the comments in reaction to the episode.

"What was that like for you?"

"I'm actually, I'm pretty low key on all social media," he says. "So, that's probably the only time I've ever had explicit haters."

Jonathan sounds introspective and refreshingly self-aware. Of course, I had thought the same thing when I had interviewed him before his conversation with Emma. Still, his humility gives me the confidence to keep pursuing this idea, which means there is one last call I need to make.

◉

"Hello?" says a voice, adorned in an Irish accent.

"Hey, K?" I ask, hoping that I'm on the phone with the right person.

"Can you hear me?" her voice cracks through the phone.

"I can hear you," I report. "Can you hear me?"

"I can indeed."

"Oh my God. Wonderful," I say, truly delighted that this is finally working out. "How are you?"

"I'm conscious, caffeinated, and clothed, so we're doing good."

Between K's accent and her aptitude for alliteration, I feel comfortable with her already. Truthfully, I had no idea what to expect when I sent her a message a few days earlier. Out of the many comments levied at Jonathan, from the one that called him "a simpleton" to the one that said, "fuck you very much, bud" and even the one that diagnosed him as "almost psychopathic," it was K's comment that stood out to me: "I was infuriated by Jon all day and I had to come here to talk about it. His ignorance perfectly distills that brand of 'smile' denial people use to dismiss survivors to their faces. He has no idea what he's talking about. Jon, if you're reading this, I hope you're eaten alive by wild dogs."

Today, just as I had vetted Jonathan for Emma's safety, here I am doing the same for him: talking to a woman who wished for Jonathan's death by canine, and determining whether or not I feel comfortable introducing them. I can almost definitively say that the answer is a resounding "yes," but I need to do my due diligence to make sure.

K, I learn, is "a bit Irish, a bit Canadian, a bit of a writer." Or "just your average bi-ped living on the planet." She describes herself as an introvert who takes walks by the sea and dabbles in music, writing, and book design. "Kind of just media tinkering, I suppose."

She recounts how she had listened to Emma and Jonathan's conversation while she was at work and the more she heard Jonathan not getting it, the "angrier and angrier" she got. In fact, she became so enraged that she went home and reactivated her Facebook account just to comment on the episode. "No small feat," she proclaims. "I hate Facebook."

"So, K," I begin, "with love and respect in my heart, what crawled under your skin so much that you told Jonathan that you hope he's eaten alive by wild dogs?"

"Basically, it was a situation where I felt Jon was trifling with a pain, the scope of which he didn't comprehend or respect, not just for Emma but for anyone out there who's listening. For myself, one of the worst things about this entire topic is that feeling of not only did someone kind of break into my body, the body you're born with, these fingers, toes, this thing you thought was yours, completely, intrinsically, until someone taught you very harshly and suddenly it was not yours. So, you have that capital T trauma. *That* kind of pain."

I often marvel at the way total strangers will open up to me on these calls in the most brutal and vulnerable ways as if I'm a close confidant.

K explains that being disbelieved as a survivor by "your parents, or someone you trust like the police, a teacher, a pastor, whatever" is "the most fucking infuriating, disempowering, horrific thing," so Jonathan's skepticism of Emma's claim hit her particularly hard.

When I ask K if she worries that speaking to Jonathan in such an extreme way will alienate him from coming to the table, pushing him away when she might want to pull him closer, she tells me that on some days she's able to approach this subject calmly, while on others she is unable to translate her rage into productive conversation.

"I basically survived a bunch of shit, most of what I don't remember, as a six-year-old," K says.

"I just missed that. You said as a six-year-old?" I ask, hoping I misheard.

"As a six-year-old," K confirms.

A lump forms in my throat.

"We don't have to go into that if you're not comfortable," I pipe up, stumbling on my words. I don't want to mine her memory for past trauma, nor do I want to lead her to an interrogation. But I'm here to listen if she wants to share.

"I just want to be upfront," she declares with confidence.

As our call winds down, I get the sense that this idea might work out after all.

"I just want to say for the record, I'm not actually looking to murder Jonathan. Just so everybody knows I'm not going to go out and kill a guy," K says with a laugh.

While I am thrilled to get this confirmation from K herself, I never suspected that this was a risk. Plus, now that I've completed the final piece of the puzzle, it's time to schedule a call.

◎

I am alone at my dining room table. Typically, when recording a moderated call, one participant has been with me while we call the other guest, but this time all three of us—Jonathan, K, and me—are scattered around the continent, waiting by our phones.

After getting Emma's blessing, gauging Jonathan's comfort, and vetting K's safety, I've finally scheduled a time when I can introduce Jonathan and K to each other, and as I sit here in front of two computers, a microphone, and a mess of wires, I feel like some sort of old-school switchboard operator, ready to plug inputs into outputs and press a series of blinking buttons, all so I can connect two people who are thousands of miles apart.

I look at the clock. It's 7:59 P.M. in New York City. It's dark out, but this is the only time that had worked for all three of our scattered time zones. *One more minute.* A wave of worry comes over me, as it often does in this final moment. *Am I just inviting a redux of Jonathan's conversation with Emma? Will K now be led to the interrogation booth, too? Will Jonathan endure another onslaught of listener feedback?* I do my best to quiet these thoughts by reminding myself that I don't have to release this episode if it doesn't go well. Which, I worry, will probably be the case.

8:00 P.M. *It's time.* I dial their numbers and wait.

"Hello?" says Jonathan.

"Hello?" says K, almost simultaneously.

Our hemispheric triangle is finally complete.

"Jonathan, you are on the phone with K. K, you are on the phone with Jonathan. And now we're all here together," I say, dutifully performing my switchboard operator role.

"Whaddup," K says.

"Hi, K," Jonathan responds.

I invite them to get to know each other and they exchange brief facts about themselves—hobbies and hometowns and jobs and goals, as if nothing ever happened between them, and they're simply strangers getting acquainted with each other. I briefly imagine what a government surveillance agency might think if they were surreptitiously listening in on this call. *Casual work acquaintances doing a getting-to-know-you exercise*, they might write down in their notes before moving onto their next target.

"K, let's actually start with you," I begin. "Why don't you explain to Jonathan why you wrote this?"

"Initially when I wrote this comment I didn't know you were going to read it. I thought you were off in the ether somewhere," K admits. "But yeah, when I listened to that episode, it really got to me."

"And, Jonathan," I say, redirecting my attention to him, "what did it feel like to read something like that?"

"Well, I guess initially when I read it, it was sort of a bit shocking," he says. "I'm not on social media that much, and that's definitely the most extreme thing anybody's ever said directed at me."

In an attempt to lighten the mood, I share with Jonathan the trivia fact that K reactivated her Facebook account just to write this comment. They both laugh.

"In a way, it's an honor, K!" he jokes.

This is going well, but I remind myself to not get too confident. After all, I had thought Emma and Jonathan's call was going well, too, and that turned into a cross-examination. The lower I keep my hopes, I figure, the less chance I have to be disappointed.

"What was Jonathan saying in the episode that really got to you?" I ask K, wondering how much she'll be willing to share with him.

"I went through some nasty shit as a kid," she states. "The thing that I craved was: I needed to be seen and understood. I just needed to see somebody and have them say to me, 'Yeah. That was fucked up. That shouldn't have happened. That was wrong.' When someone just flat out is like, 'Well, I don't know. I don't believe you. There's not enough evidence.' It's such a disempowering thing and it's salt on the wound."

I ask Jonathan how this sits with him.

"I mean, I don't really have any moral authority. I don't think I'm any kind of god or all-knowing—I'm a lowly evolved primate like everybody else. I was going off what I read on the internet," Jonathan replies.

His tone isn't defensive, but almost deferential. This sounds like such a different Jonathan than the one who spoke to Emma a few months ago. While that Jonathan might have plumbed for answers, and dug for proof, this Jonathan is closely listening. And whereas before he needed every detail explained to him, now he's holding space for K to share as much of her story as she feels comfortable to share.

"It's not just you as a person, Jon," K begins softly. Beneath her words I can hear the early construction of an empathy cushion. "It's everyone who's expressed something similar to you. So you stop becoming Jon, you become like this amalgamation of everyone who's hurt me in that way. On my best days, I would love to be reasonable, patient, and explain it and link you the story so you can understand exactly what people have gone through and see what their experience is through their own eyes, because I think we can all relate to stories done that way. But I mean on my worst days, and worst moment like this, it's just so primal. There's only directing it in certain ways. It's so incapacitating, that kind of rage."

Just as Emma had offered grace to Jonathan, K is now doing the same by softly acknowledging that Jonathan isn't the system but simply one of its unofficially elected representatives.

And with this parallel I notice something else. Just as Emma had become a symbol to Jonathan—of the fate that might befall good, innocent men—Jonathan then became a symbol to K of all the people who didn't believe her. Hearing K separate Jonathan the Person from Jonathan the Symbol reminds me, once again, what these conversations— and *all* conversations—do best: They separate the person from the system, the part from the whole, the micro from the macro.

Still, I worry that just as he did with Emma, Jonathan will meet K's empathy cushion with a conversational riptide.

"I'm definitely sorry that it made you feel that way," Jonathan replies. I brace myself for a *but*. "I didn't say it wanting to make anybody feel that way. I think it might come from, just, ignorance around it that I have."

I wait, but there is no riptide. He provides no asterisk. Just a pure, undistilled apology.

"I appreciate that," K replies. "I fully recognize that pinning all that stuff to you [. . .] dehumanizes you and it's not fair."

"I get why it would be triggering for somebody who's been through it," Jonathan says.

"Well, I appreciate that, man. Thank you."

Jonathan is apologizing without caveat. The two of them have found a rhythm all their own, and I am thrilled to be a third wheel that just happens to be along for the ride. While I'm thrilled to sit back and hear them connect with each other, I try to use this momentum to revisit the subject that brought them together in the first place: false accusations.

"Jonathan, we would share your loathing of people who accuse falsely of rape," K begins, "because, I mean, first of all, you're putting an innocent person through the meat grinder. So, fuck you. And then secondly, it reinforces that myth that . . . It's almost the first thing people bring up when they hear an allegation. So, ultimately, if people make false allegations knowingly as some sort of, I don't know, power move or vengeance or whatever, it ultimately helps other rapists for other survivors to walk free."

"Yeah. I totally agree," Jonathan responds. "I think, just to take a step back, I do think it is very, very rare that somebody does falsely accuse." Not only is there no conversational riptide but Jonathan is actually doubling down on his agreement with K.

He continues, "Listening to it five or six times like I have the first interview, I get why people would . . . I did sometimes sound a little bit unhinged, especially for a person who's been through it."

I had no idea that he re-listened to his conversation with Emma so many times, but I'm pleased to hear that he had.

"I have to say, I am sorry, Jonathan, that I came at you so hard," K offers genuinely.

"Well, I definitely accept your apology one hundred percent. For you, for everybody else that listened to it that maybe had a similar triggering experience, I apologize. I mean I think in the truest sense, I was pretty ignorant, and it only got worse as the thing went on. This has made me think about it in a whole new way. I know it might sound ignorant to say, but it made me think about it in ways I didn't even know to think about it."

His last sentence echoes in my head. *It made me think about it in ways I didn't even know to think about it.* I may not yet understand what magic led to this transformation, but I'm deeply grateful for it.

"I'm very glad you were not eaten alive by wild dogs or eaten dead by wild dogs," K begins. "It's been really cathartic to actually talk to you. So, I appreciate that you took the time to come on here. That means a lot, so thank you."

"And I appreciate you, too," Jonathan replies. "It's always good to make a new friend where at one time maybe it didn't seem possible. So, I think that's a good thing as well."

"Likewise," K says. "Be prepared for shit posts and memes." She laughs, at first in a cartoonishly maniacal cackle, then in a gentle, genuine one.

"I'm ready!" Jonathan says.

After we say our goodbyes, I hang up the call and confirm that the recordings are saved. Then, I mindlessly stand up, walk to the couch, lie down, stare at the ceiling, and try to process what just happened.

This was the dramatic transformation that I had been hoping for, the *Fixer Upper* ending that I had been dreaming of, just a few months later than I had anticipated. Like those new homeowners, marveling at their open atrium and seeing how a space that was once one thing, dramatically became something else, I am in awe of what just happened.

Jonathan seems to have truly *changed*, but how? What made this different from all my other episodes? I have certainly seen inspirational moments before—I've heard guests reconsider their preconceived notions; I've listened to them soften on their once hardline stances. In moments of silence, I've sensed them recognize how something they wrote may have been more hurtful than they had intended, but I'd never heard someone sound truly *different*. Just a few months earlier Jonathan had been firmly resisting Emma's story, and tonight he carefully listened to a new person tell *their* account of sexual assault, and instead of meeting her with doubt he met her with a listening ear.

I wonder if maybe I did something wrong on his call with Emma. Had this Jonathan been there all along and with better worded questions I could have accessed him? Maybe now that Jonathan was the recipient of the comment, and not the author, he was able to be more open? Maybe I had just caught him on a bad day? As I cycle through all the possible factors that may have led to his transformation, the only one that makes any sense seems too simple. Could that really be it? Was it just *time*?

◎

Transformation, as it turns out, isn't as tidy as home renovation shows make us think it is. *Fixer Upper* is far from the only culprit. Television shows, movies, and books suggest that full arcs of evolution are completed in a neatly contained period of time. But in all of these media, we forget that real time is collapsed. Hidden. Edited out. To be fair, I condense time on my podcast, too. I edit down my phone calls to be suitable for the listeners. Who wants to hear a two-hour phone call, when a forty-minute edit tells the same story with the same arcs? We collapse time in service of entertainment. And this is precisely why I love *Fixer Upper*. It hides time between invisible edit points, often documenting work that takes months, even years, and compacts it into a tight forty-three-minute confection for our viewing ease.

Reality, unfortunately, doesn't work this way. There are no edits for life. No cuts for evolution. No speed-throughs. No montages over fun songs. Problems are not magically solved after an ad break.

Real change must happen in real time, in the messy and unorganized way that life demands. Change, we are told through stories, looks like a person completely abandoning everything they believe and adopting a new "correct" way of thinking. It's a person suddenly leaving behind their old life and picking up an entirely new one.

Real time can't fit in the tidy containers of popular storytelling. Unfortunately, popular storytelling is how we understand ourselves and the world around us. It sets the standards that we in turn set for ourselves. And it is this tension between reality and fantasy, between real time and edited time, that creates what I can only think to call the Makeover Illusion, that subconscious expectation that transformation can happen quickly and in montage.

Real-time storytelling is boring. No one wants to watch a six-thousand-hour livestream of a home renovation. We want to see the highlights. And so, we get home renovation shows instead. But human beings aren't television houses. Our beliefs cannot be made over in forty-three minutes; we can only move at the excruciating pace of real time.

It occurs to me that perhaps my acquaintance, the one who pressed me for the "point" of the show in an email, has been deceived by the Makeover Illusion himself. That, through no fault of his own, he can't comprehend why someone would create a project that features conversations that are far closer to real time than they are to television time.

Of course, time itself doesn't guarantee change. "Time heals all wounds" is one of those beautiful idioms that could easily become a meaningless slogan, doomed to an eternal rest in the catchphrase graveyard right beside "love trumps hate." Both phrases are helpful reminders that take powerful concepts—love and time—and essentially distill them into one of those automated robotic vacuums that simply takes care of our messes while we sit back and relax. But neither phrase acknowledges the work it takes to put those powerful concepts into practice. Love doesn't trump hate without action, and time doesn't heal all wounds without medical attention. It needs bandages, antibiotic ointments, and sometimes stitches, too.

Jonathan's ideas didn't soften on our second call simply because enough hours passed between one call and the next, or because some magic number of sunrises and sunsets had permitted him to rethink his position. It happened because he let Emma's words sink in after their call ended. It happened because he listened back to their conversation "five or six times." It happened because he actually listened to K, even after she had told him she hoped he was "eaten alive by wild dogs." It happened because K was able to separate Jonathan the Person from Jonathan the Symbol and speak to him as the former and not the latter.

By using *Fixer Upper* as a barometer for my success I was setting myself up for failure. It was unrealistic of me to expect Jonathan—or anyone—to change on a single phone call. None of us can instantaneously evolve after being introduced to a brand-new idea. I certainly can't. Only with time and space could Jonathan renovate his thoughts and demolish his old walls of resistance.

Radical change does not happen in the course of a single phone call. It does not happen because a conversation ends on a happy note. It happens because someone is willing to listen, someone is able to reach them, and a bridge was created for them to meet.

What is the point of this? my acquaintance asked in his email. Well, I finally have an answer.

The point, I want to kindly tell him, is simply to build that bridge. To make it as safe and comfortable as possible for those who are willing to cross it. The point is to record their meeting on that bridge and share it in all its messy, beautiful, and challenging glory with the hopes that it will help others reset their expectations from the impossible standards of television time to the humbling pace of real time—or at least something much closer to it than a dazzling home improvement show.

10
trash

A blank word document stares at me. The cursor blinks impatiently, mocking me as it flashes on and off. On the ground are scraps of paper—copious notes, printouts of articles, and transcripts of phone calls with my guests—organized into piles that I'm generously choosing to call "chapters." I am writing my book. Well, "writing" is also a generous term. I am *thinking* about how to write my book. The book about my social experiment and all that I've learned from it. The book whose first due date was over a year ago, and whose second due date has also come and gone. The book that I fear is doomed to never exist.

It is late June of 2020. Almost two years have passed since my call with Jonathan and K. I know that this book should have been finished by now. In fact, this is the very month that it was initially meant to be released. It's not that I've been busy with the podcast. On the contrary, I've intentionally produced fewer episodes to focus on writing. Nor is it because writing is hard. Of course, it *is* hard—sometimes virtually impossible—but it's famously hard for everyone; I am not unique. Confusingly, it's not even because I haven't been working on it. I have. Diligently. But all of that work has yielded nothing more than a dense cache of notes.

I don't know why this is happening, I confess during walks with friends. *It just doesn't make sense,* I wearily complain to Todd each night. And in emails to my editor, I optimistically promise *It's coming, it's coming.* Truthfully, though, in my most private moments I have a strong suspicion of what's holding me back: the paralyzing fear that I will be publicly shamed for writing this book.

Many refer to the source of my fear as "cancel culture," but this term seems to mean a different thing to each person who uses it. Some employ the term to identify the punitive actions of the progressive left. Others celebrate it as a necessary populist tool to take down the Bad Guys, and a third group claims it doesn't even exist. "There is no such thing," they argue. "It's 'consequence culture,' not 'cancel culture.'"

I have silently disagreed with each of these assertions for a while now.

For one thing, "cancel culture" is not exclusive to a political ideology. Nor has it ever been. As a teenager I watched conservatives burn the CDs of the Chicks—then called the Dixie Chicks—after their lead singer expressed distaste for President Bush. Colin Kaepernick was all but excommunicated from the NFL after he began kneeling during the national anthem as an act of solidarity with Black victims of state violence. I was even *at* the RNC, covering it for my job, when Senator Ted Cruz was booed by his fellow Republicans for not supporting then-candidate Trump. Plus, pinning the entire practice of "cancellation" exclusively on a mob of progressives often confuses a righteous reconsideration of history with "cancellation." Christopher Columbus isn't "cancelled"; people are simply reconsidering the legacy of a man who terrorized an entire population of human beings.

Additionally, "cancel culture" doesn't just go after the Bad Guys, however comforting that notion may be. While it is capable of taking down individuals who have committed offenses universally agreed to be "Very Bad"—like serial sexual abusers, perpetrators of racist hate crimes, and vitriolic bosses—many of its targets have committed wrongs far less egregious. I have watched private citizens be shunned for tweeting a poorly thought out joke, social media users mocked for the crime of having a "bad take," and other individuals be taken to task for simply being "cringe."

I find it most challenging, though, to articulate my disagreement with those who claim it doesn't exist, as this group includes many of my smartest friends and other members of my ideological tribe. While I find it valid to question what the word "cancel" actually means when many "cancelled" people have gone on to enjoy continued professional success after a so-called "cancellation," I don't think that serves as automatic proof that it doesn't exist. Yes, a celebrated comedian may have booked a lucrative comedy special after fielding criticism for transphobic jokes and a Hollywood director who infamously went on racist, antisemitic, and abusive tirades may still be working, but just because the elite don't face the same consequences as others doesn't mean "cancel culture" isn't real. It just means that it doles out its punishment unevenly.

While the exact name of this phenomenon is still in the process of being defined—or more accurately, *re*defined as the idea of "cancelling" was popularized in Black internet spaces before it was adopted into the mainstream—I know there is a culture of *something*. And that something terrifies me. Years ago, the journalist Jon Ronson identified it as shame. "We were at the start of a great renaissance of public shaming," Ronson wrote in his seminal 2015 book *So You've Been Publicly Shamed*. "When we deployed shame, we were utilizing an immensely powerful tool. It was coercive, borderless, and increasing in speed and influence."

I fear the looming threat of this "immensely powerful tool"—this culture of shame—every day. So much so that it has been nearly impossible to write anything, much less a book in which I will commit the very transgressions that seem to sometimes incur its wrath.

◎

When I pitched my book to potential publishers in November of 2018, some asked how long it would take to finish and each time, I replied with total confidence: "I'm a fast writer and I can have it to you in six months."

This was bold—not to mention humiliating in retrospect—but I wasn't worried because the story I wanted to tell was clear in my head: I would begin by recounting my conversation with Josh, end on my call with Jonathan and K, and in between I would share all that I'd learned from my ongoing social experiment. *Easy.* But when I finally sat down to write, I became overwhelmed by the permanence that a book would grant my ideas. Sure, all of my videos were still searchable online, as were my podcast episodes, and I understood that every tweet, Facebook post, and Instagram picture I had ever shared would live forever on a server somewhere, but there was something different, almost holier, about a book. A book was a public document essentially written in stone and I came to see it as a precious, unerasable record of my thoughts and opinions. Once published, there would be no going back. Which meant that everything I shared in its pages had to be factually correct, emotionally honest, but most important, morally inscrutable, which is to say that it needed to be firmly rooted on the Right Side of History so that both the book and I would be resistant to shame.

While shame wasn't exclusive to any one political group (see above), I knew that the shame I needed to protect myself from was that of my *own* tribe, my own fellow progressives. It would be one thing for my ideas to be disparaged by those who already disagreed with me, but it would be uniquely heartbreaking to see it ripped apart by my own people. I suppose this fear was strange considering that I was setting out to write a book that would celebrate talking to people who hated me—or *seemed* to hate me—but online shame was a different beast than online hate. Online hate certainly stung, but I believed it said more about the person who sent it than the person they sent it to. Shame, on the other hand, seemed to cast blame solely on the recipient, marking them as a violator of community standards for doing something "unacceptable." So, in the early stages of the writing process, I resolved to actively keep watch on social media as a way to know what was and was not acceptable in the hopes of making my ideas shame-proof.

Day after day I sat in the bleachers of the internet and took it all in. Soon enough the users I followed, the people *they* followed, and the various media that all of them shared became a constantly updating moral compass whose many takes, opinions, and observations became memos from an unofficial focus group that would help guide the ideas I planned to share in my book—a book about radical empathy, the importance of conversation, and the humanity I found in my digital detractors.

Not even a week after I had sent my editor my first piece of writing, Amnesty International and Element AI published their study, the one that found that women of color—especially Black women—receive a disproportionate amount of online abuse. In the official press release announcing the study, Milena Marin, Amnesty's Senior Advisor for Tactical Research, said, "Twitter's failure to crack down on this problem means it is contributing to the silencing of already marginalized voices." How could I write a book about the virtues of speaking to internet detractors when hard data was clearly pointing to how impossible such a project might be for others? How could I publicly celebrate the act of building bridges online without looking completely out-of-touch? Wouldn't writing this book be flaunting my own privilege in the face of so many who didn't have the energy or time to even imagine such a social experiment?

I did my best to forge ahead, though, and was already writing loose sketches of chapters when I came across an interview with Lindy West, the writer who had famously spoken to her own detractor on a now-iconic installment of the radio show *This American Life* years before I even began *Conversations with People Who Hate Me*. I remember listening with my jaw on the floor as West calmly confronted a man who harassed her on Twitter by making a fake account with the likeness of her late father. I had long regarded her as a vanguard of the form, but when I clicked to open the link to her interview, I saw that she had a new position. "At this point, in 2019," West told the journalist Joe Berkowitz, "I have less interest in redeeming internet trolls." Even though I knew that she was only speaking for herself, I couldn't help but think that this quote was speaking directly to me, as if to say *Dylan, it's time to move on*. Was it?

Over the following months my fingers grew increasingly resistant to typing anything that went against the edicts of my unofficial focus group. If I attempted to express anything that sounded too hopeful, my hands would stage a protest and refuse. This resistance continued, and when my first deadline—May 28, 2019—came and went, I knew I had to change my approach.

The memos from my million-member focus group kept streaming in. Friends clapped back at public gestures of unity, well-meaning pleas for kindness were swiftly mocked by people I respected, and calls for empathy were labeled "irresponsible." As challenging as it was to see the core elements of my project derided by some of the sharpest and wittiest members of my unofficial focus group, I needed to find a way to concentrate, so I rented a desk at a writing center, transferred all of my notes to index cards, reorganized them, started fresh, and by the fall of 2019 I had a stack of notes that I was sure would magically transform into a book in no time.

One Sunday in early October of 2019, as I was polishing an outline for the book, I came across a picture of Ellen DeGeneres sitting beside George W. Bush at a football game, engaged in a friendly chat. This image was sweet. There was a gay woman laughing at a joke with a former president who publicly fought to "protect the institution of marriage" between a man and a woman. Even without knowing what they were laughing about, this image reminded me of my own moments like these. That time Josh stepped on a Lego after explaining why he believed homosexuality to be a sin and I couldn't help but break out into a smile. Or when E and I joked about my misuse of the word "lunging" right after he called pride parades "pointless." I thought of the brief respite when Emma and Jonathan had a funny exchange about whether or not she could yet call him "Jon" in the middle of their difficult phone call about her sexual assault. These flashes of humanity were not only helpful, but inevitable. The talk show host and the former president may have been larger-than-life avatars, but their shared moment reflected a rare kind of relationship that I had come to know well. Then, I started to see the reaction it elicited.

One friend labeled this kindness "unforgivable."

"Do fuck off," wrote another person in response to Ellen's subsequent explanation of the picture.

But there was more nuanced criticism, too. "In our current political moment, niceness no longer appears to be a cure-all. And uncritical niceness may no longer be a viable brand," Constance Grady wrote for *Vox.* "In many ways, it feels as though niceness is no longer enough, as though it might perhaps even be slightly immoral."

Though I wasn't speaking to former heads of state on *Conversations with People Who Hate Me*, nor had any of my guests sent a country to an unjust war, was I promoting "uncritical niceness" by extending empathy to strangers who had hurt me online? Was I doing something "slightly immoral" by creating a space for people to calmly and kindly speak to each other? It appeared as though every public gesture of unity was interpreted as a mandate for all. Was I issuing this mandate, too?

These messages from my focus group were clear: radical empathy, unity, and even dialogue itself seemed to be social sins in my corner of the internet and each time I received one of these memos it felt as though a "wanted" sign had been posted all over the town square. When I stepped closer to inspect it, I noticed that the sketch of the suspect looked just like me. Perhaps my focus group was trying to tell me that empathy *was* endorsement, after all.

By January of 2020, once I soared past the second deadline my editor had graciously given me, I stopped writing altogether, so consumed by the fear that I might commit the Wrong Thought to paper, publish that Wrong Thought, and then be mercilessly mocked for doing so. If at first I regarded my million-member focus group as an intimidating but brilliant guide, I eventually came to see it as a terrifying force that might deploy a wave of shame against me—which I began to think of as a shame army. Rather than writing, I opted to closely study the patterns, methods, and movements of these roving battalions in the hopes of protecting myself from them, as if knowledge would immunize me from their clutches. Here is what I observed:

Shame armies depended on soldiers to do their bidding. These fighters enlisted at a moment's notice, all for a variety of reasons. Some seemed to join in so they could be part of the joke, others appeared to be genuinely interested in publicly planting their flag on the right side of history, while a few seemed to not realize that by expressing an opinion about a trending topic they were unwittingly donning a battle uniform. No two armies were alike, because each one was composed of a different group of volunteers that would disband after each battle. Some of them were my friends, and they looked almost unrecognizable when I saw them on the battlefield. "Suck my whole dick," an otherwise soft-spoken and intelligent acquaintance wrote about a television pundit's tasteless joke.

The weapons these soldiers used varied, too. Some of them were sharp steel arrows that were terrifying even to read. "ELECTRIC CHAIR," I saw in response to an upcoming memoir. Other munitions, however, were softer like "big yikes," "this ain't it chief," "so you've decided to tweet this here's why you shouldn't have," "well that didn't age well," and other phrases that encapsulated the internet's holy trinity of cynicism, apathy, and dismissal. Considered independently these were nothing more than rubber bullets—harmless and often funny— but the power of shame armies was less in the quality of their weaponry, and more in the quantity of weapons they deployed. After all, it was through their numbers that they could tip the scales—whether by downvoting a post, disliking a YouTube video en masse, or giving a tweet more replies than likes. *Ratio* became a verb.

The size of a shame army also varied. It seemed like any given army could be composed of millions of social media users, five, two hundred and twelve, or anything in between. Unhelpfully, the activity of these brigades would be reported with oversimplified headlines that linguistically transformed any size army into the entirety of the social media platform it operated on. "Twitter Is Mad About *This*" "Social Media Had Some Thoughts About *That*." Sometimes it just credited the entire World Wide Web, too. "The Internet Is Mad About *Some-*

thing." My mind would do this as well, inaccurately labeling a group of twelve people "everyone" and misguidedly wondering why the whole world had decided to take aim at, say, the animators of a videogame movie adaptation. Shame troops grew more powerful in my imagination because of this uncanny ability the internet had to distort scale.

Shame armies targeted transgressors, and each of these targets came to be known as the internet's "main character" for their central position as the human punching bag of the day. What qualified as a transgression, however, was hard to pin down. Sometimes it was an action that was universally agreed to be Bad and Wrong. Other times it was the simple sin of daring to express sincerity online. "This shot is brilliant and should be shown in any film study class," a man earnestly tweeted in reference to a scene in the *Game of Thrones* series finale. Within hours, his harmless observation became a meme, its text copied and pasted over stills from campy musicals, goofy effects from old films, and out-of-context screenshots from other television shows. "I didn't enjoy going viral on this," he wrote after deleting his original tweet.

Misdeeds of all severity levels played at the same volume thanks to the internet's relentlessness. Shame, unnecessarily cruel mockery, righteous critique, and collective justice began to blend together into my vague and reductive observation that "the internet is mean." In the time of writing my book—or, *trying* to write my book—I watched shame armies target the following transgressors: authors of articles with "bad takes," authors of tweets with "bad takes," a barber who gave uneven haircuts, a man who launched a racist and xenophobic tirade at a Black woman on a train, a man who made jerk chicken with too little seasoning, a leftist journalist who appeared on a conservative media outlet, a comedian who made a joke about a deceased rapper, a YouTuber who allegedly liked Beyoncé for clout, an entrepreneur who hunted endangered animals, a comedian who made transphobic jokes, a man who held up encouraging notecards for his wife while she was in labor, a news outlet that wrote a sexist headline about a female rock icon, two Latina women who were announced as Super Bowl halftime performers, a journalist who profiled a prominent conservative, a wrestling organization that ended a match badly, a journalist who received negative student feedback from a summer course they taught, the digital effects team of a popular movie-musical adaptation, a private citizen who didn't like a YA author's work, and then, in retaliation, said YA author for calling out said private citizen, an educator who shared a template for expressing emotional burnout, a contestant on a reality show who sometimes spoke in an affected baby voice, and a teenage activist who was perceived to be too earnest.

The consequences of being targeted by a shame army seemed to range from a digital slap on the wrist to job loss. The consequences didn't necessarily correspond to the crime.

There were people, though, that shame armies seemed to spare, a select group who were furiously protected "at all costs." This included celebrities who were fluent in the language of the internet, celebrities who were endearingly *not* fluent in the language of the internet but tried to speak it anyway, celebrities whose lack of digital presence allowed them to become blank screens upon which adoring onlookers could project their own thoughts and ideas, anthropomorphized fictional characters from action-movie franchises, K-pop groups, underrated actresses of a certain age, and the Phillies hockey mascot Gritty. Random civilians could be elevated to this status, too. "Just saw someone put two pieces of pizza together and eat it like a sandwich so, that guy for president 2020?" an actress tweeted out. Members of this protected class seemed like untouchable demigods and were adorned with phrases like GOAT (Greatest of All Time), queen, and king. To mock them was often a transgression itself.

If shame armies transformed social media into a battlefield, then it was one that existed in conjunction with a human stock exchange where an individual's worth was determined by their spot on the spectrum between transgressor and GOAT. The value of an untouchable demigod could plummet at the mere suggestion of a misstep, and shame soldiers could increase their own value by dragging an offender in an entertaining way.

As 2020 unfolded, the rare confluence of a global pandemic and an overdue uprising for racial justice cast shame armies in a new light. Maybe, I thought, they were vital social tools capable of bending the moral arc of the universe toward justice. Maybe they were, indeed, better than the flawed criminal justice system some claimed they were meant to replace. I found it thrilling to watch them in action when I disagreed with the wrongdoer. In these moments I believed them to be the Voice of the People, noble proletariat uprisings. But my optimism would invariably fade whenever I saw a shame army target a person whose offense was so minor, knowing that I was powerless to shield them from the firing squad. With so many soldiers enlisting at such a fast rate, their aim often became sloppy. Errors seemed to be written off as "tough luck." Perhaps the flaws of this new criminal justice system were nothing more than a remix of the old ones.

In their righteous quest to tear down problematic systems, it seemed as if these infantries were only interested in taking down individual people instead. They went after the transgressor as if they *were* the system itself. So-called "Karens" *became* white entitlement, a prominent television creator *was* nepotism, and the celebrities who sang the song "Imagine" *were* privilege itself. It was as if shame soldiers knew that they couldn't mock a social ill, "ratio" a broken healthcare system, or tell centuries-old racism "big yikes." Of course, they *could*, but there didn't seem to be a point. Shame armies were out for blood, so why would they waste their arrows on something that couldn't bleed?

Closely observing the patterns and activity of these squads afforded me the ability to catch glimpses of shame cadets taking aim at their targets with pride, and this pride reminded me of the glory I would feel when leveling a Goliath with my videos. I remember the rush that I got from a coin haul and the honor that came with aligning myself with the right side of history so publicly. As hard as it was to admit, I recognized myself in them. In the same way that I would sometimes look into the lens of a camera years earlier and aim my biting jokes at whatever opponent I had identified that day—thinking that by doing so I was taking down conservatism itself—now I was seeing others do the same exact thing over and over again. Here I was judging these soldiers for their tactics, trembling in fear that they might catch me, conveniently forgetting that I was a decorated veteran of this very war. And then, a second realization: I wasn't observing a strange new social phenomenon, I was simply watching new players compete in an updated version of the game I had once dominated. Just as debate turned conversation into a sport, shame turned justice into a spectacle.

There were, however, two key differences.

For one thing, in my days of this game it seemed the directive was to attack the "other side," now it was to attack each *other*. Fights over police abolition versus police reform seemed far more common to me than cross-ideological debates about gun rights. I saw more jabs taken at Democratic primary candidates than I did toward President Trump. Calling out a person who tweeted an overly sentimental wish for world peace appeared to be more worthwhile than calling out someone who said, "Make America Great Again." Maybe this was because I had been sorted into an algorithmic echo chamber where I was only seeing like-minded people, or maybe after realizing that our arrows couldn't reach the other side, we decided to point them at each other instead.

The second difference was more personal. Whereas before I was an MVP, this time I was sitting in the bleachers, watching from the sidelines. My old stomping ground now felt like foreign territory and I was newly aware that the same digital weapons I had once wielded could just as easily be used against me. From this new vantage point I was able to see a terrifying consequence of the game that I couldn't appreciate before: There was no clear path to redemption. Shame armies demanded apologies from transgressors, and then refused to accept them. Worse, there seemed to be a trend of mocking apologies in the comment sections *of* those apologies. "Fixed it for you," some would reply, along with a screenshot of the apology in question, annotated with scribbled edits. Sometimes these corrections were valuable pointers in how to truly take accountability, while other times they seemed more like opportunities to further humiliate the culprit and entertain fellow soldiers.

What terrified me most, though, was the finality of the language of shame. Transgressors were called such absolute terms as "monster" and "disgusting." Onlookers urged other shame fighters to "finish" or "destroy" the wrongdoer of the moment. But the label that really got to me was "trash." The word felt ubiquitous. It was the weapon of choice. There was something so hauntingly absolute about it. With just five letters it rendered the transgressor worthless and disposable.

Perhaps this extreme language was nothing more than the by-product of a digital age that rewarded hyperbole and jokes, but what was it doing to our psyches when we referred to our fellow human beings as "trash"? How did rendering other people as disposable affect our understanding of each other? How did it affect our understanding of ourselves?

This was quite a scene that I was witnessing day after day. And sitting in these bleachers, with all of these questions running through my head; as I watched shame armies instantaneously form around me; as transgressors were sent to the dump, never to return; as systems were confused for people and people were confused for punching bags, I had to somehow write a book that advocated for unity and empathy and understanding. A book about a project that saw humanity in both the outlaws who were regarded as trash *and* the soldiers who dismissed them as such. A book that I was sure would mark me as trash, too.

◉

A blank word document stares at me. The cursor blinks impatiently, mocking me as it flashes on and off.

My book contract asks for an eighty-thousand-word manuscript, and given this new version of the game—or rather, my new position in it—that feels like eighty thousand opportunities to mess up. Eighty thousand different ways that I might become the main character of the day. Eighty thousand chances for a shame army to dismiss me as useless garbage.

As I sit here, I know that I should be devoting all of my creative energy to typing my first sentence. Instead, I can't stop rehearsing how each potential phrasing of every single idea might play in the public square. This is less writing than it is calculation. I am trying to devise the perfect combination of words that will let me pass through the public square undetected. If I imagine a sentence, my mind then goes to the inevitable fallout if that sentence is "wrong." What will I say to the teenager who replies with a "this ain't it chief" on an Instagram post about my book's release date? How will I handle being the main character when someone finds a sentence that I should have written differently? How long will it take to get over an ideologically-aligned stranger responding to my book's presale link with the meme "you decided to write this book, here's why you shouldn't have"—ironically with no actual explanation as to *why* I shouldn't have written it, only the announcement that I have made a grievous mistake by doing so? How will I tell the difference between necessary criticism and shame for sport? I find myself preemptively writing Notes app apologies in my head for wrongs I don't even know I'll commit while simultaneously brainstorming comebacks to the shame soldiers who might make fun of me for the medium I've used to type my apology.

Part of me desperately wants to give up. To pay back my book advance. To quit the podcast. To never record another conversation. To never release another episode. To never do anything that would put me at risk of becoming the main character of the day.

Still, I know that I'm sitting here because I believe in what I'm doing. I'm sitting here because Josh and Frank and Adam and E and Emma and Jonathan and K and my dozens of other guests have shown me the possibility of a new model of communication, one that is restorative and loving, not punitive and shameful.

So, I force myself to write a sentence.

It's the worst sentence ever written, but a sentence, nonetheless.

Then, I force myself to extend that sentence into a paragraph.

Okay. No disaster yet.

A few hours later I'm looking at a page full of words.

Over the following days I take small steps, resisting the fear of the shame arrows while still keeping an eye on the passing soldiers so I can know their coordinates. In my breaks from writing I watch new armies form, new transgressors be targeted, and the volatile human stock exchange fluctuate wildly in response.

Then, one evening, as I finally near the end of my first draft of my first chapter, I give myself ten minutes to tweet about a recent news story. After I compose the tweet and publish it, I repeatedly refresh my notifications to make sure I didn't say anything wrong. Really, I'm on the lookout for that first sign of an incoming army—one person's dissent or skepticism—hoping that I'll be able to catch it in time and delete it.

Refresh, refresh, refresh.

When I look up, I see that I've spent an entire hour stuck in this repetitive action.

The fear of shame armies had already stolen years from me. Now I've just watched it steal another hour. And so, for the first time since creating a social media profile fourteen years ago, after devoting myself to a project that required close attention to the internet, I do something I've never done before, something I had previously thought to be unthinkable: I log off.

11
recycling

It's only been a few days of being off social media, but already I feel renewed. On my daily walks I find myself taking pictures, not of things that might appeal to my followers, but sights that are pleasing to me—a neon pink sunset, the canopy of an oak tree, the rolling hills of Prospect Park. I text these pictures to friends, and as I do, I rediscover that antiquated sensation of sharing an observation with just one person rather than every single social media user. Best of all, I'm finally writing my book. More and more every day. Without the ability to keep up with the latest shame army, I am more able to take stock of what I actually think rather than defaulting to the opinion factory of social media. While my focus is certainly better, distraction continues to plague me as I write. I am still, for better or worse, myself. But where before I would open my phone and scroll, now whenever I grow tired of writing—which still happens about once every ninety seconds—I simply look outside.

To the left of my desk is a window overlooking the lively Brooklyn avenue that my neighbors pass throughout the day, running their errands, walking their dogs, and sometimes rushing to get to wherever they need to be. I suppose this is my new, analog version of social media—and I'm coming to love it. It's an organic scroll that I can't control, a natural algorithm determined by geographic proximity. Framing this view is a honey locust tree whose leaves create a proscenium curtain and a towering black lamppost whose light turns on at sunset and off at sunrise. I love this new existence. But with this newfound consciousness, I am now acutely aware of *everything* that's happening outside, which includes a growing pile of uncollected trash at the base of the lamppost. Or, more specifically, a growing pile of paper recycling.

Recycling, like most things in New York City, is governed by a strict set of rules. First, it must be put out at the right time. On our block, recycling is collected only on Tuesday mornings. Recyclable materials also need to be presented in a certain way; glass, metals, and plastics go in one clear bag, while paper recycling goes in another. Large cardboard boxes that can't fit into clear plastic bags must be broken down and bound together with twine. And so, every Monday night we all scurry down our stairs carrying the bottles, cans, plastic tubs, old mail, and cardboard boxes we've been hoarding for the week and place them at the foot of this regal lamppost. If the recycling is either put out at the wrong time or in the wrong way, it won't be collected, so we all adhere to these rules in order to do our small part for the greater good of the planet. Someone, however, doesn't seem to know these rules, which is why I am now looking at a pile of unsightly, unbound cardboard boxes.

This is the first time I've seen these unbound boxes and I wonder if this is a frequent occurrence that I'm only just noticing after finally looking up from my phone. I try to ignore them, but that's a little challenging when I'm looking outside every minute and a half. These boxes greet me each time I step outside my front door for the daily walks I've come to love. After a few days, no one seems to be doing anything about them, so I decide to take matters into my own hands. I throw on some surgical gloves, grab a trash bag, and make my way downstairs. Apparently getting off of social media hasn't cured my aptitude for theatrics.

"Thanks for cleaning it up," the owner of the local taqueria texts me. "I can't tell you how much we clean up around the neighborhood . . . it seems like most people don't care."

I decide to interpret this kind acknowledgment of my very basic community contribution as proof that we, the Good Residents of this Fair Village, are now united against a common foe. It's Us, the Good versus Them, the Disrespectful Paper Discarders. And we will win.

The next week it happens again. If a few days ago I was peeved, now I'm officially frustrated. *Who is doing this?* I wonder as I wrestle an oversized box into a bag for the second week in a row. And just as I begin to wonder how I'll find the culprit, I notice a small white sticker, peeking out of one of the box's many sides. A delivery address. Mystery solved. The delinquent lives two buildings down from me. And now that I've unmasked this villain, I can begin plotting my revenge.

When I see yet another pile of unbound and unbagged paper recycling for a third week in a row, I resolve that this week's cleanup will be my final act of goodwill. It's time for retaliation. My mind runs wild with ideas. Next week, when it happens again, should I bring the box to their front door, shocking them that I know where they live while subtly mocking the fact that they forgot to remove the delivery tags from their boxes? Should I stand watch by my window next Monday night to catch them in the act and publicly identify them so that the whole community can learn the true identity of this villain? What if I print out a sign and affix it to the lamppost? "ATTENTION:" I imagine it reading in all caps. "PLEASE LOOK UP CITY RECYCLING REQUIREMENTS BEFORE DEPOSITING YOUR CARDBOARD BOXES HERE. THANK YOU." I will make sure to angle this sign so that it directly faces their apartment building, greeting them as they emerge with their unkempt paper. A rush of adrenaline courses through me as I picture the look on their face, humiliated that they've finally been found out. I imagine all the other neighbors—the *Good* ones, I mean—cheering me on for single-handedly ending PaperRecyclingGate once and for all.

As the fourth Tuesday approaches, it's time to put my plan in motion. But now that it's go time, I get cold feet. The idea of dumping the box on their doorstep feels too aggressive and waiting by my window to catch them in the act is too time-consuming. This leaves me with only one option: the all-caps sign. But even this feels weird. What if they see me do it? That thought alone gives me a chill of anticipatory anxiety. Plus, they live fifty feet away from me. If they know who left the sign, it'll be incredibly uncomfortable to pass them on the street. But I don't want to keep bagging their recycling. Nor do I want it cluttering the view outside my window. So, I take a marker to a blank piece of paper and opt for a different approach.

"Hey!" I write. "I live a few doors down and have noticed that your paper recycling has been untied and unbagged for the last few weeks. I've sometimes been bagging it for you but figured I'd let you know because these rules can be hard to keep straight."

I read the note over, fold it, place it in an envelope, walk downstairs, and deliver it to their mailbox. After weeks of fuming at them, and days of scheming, this solution took just four minutes. This simple act of writing a note and sending it to them privately, releases my mounting frustration. And with this newfound peace I can finally see two things: One, my hyperawareness of shame armies didn't immunize me from becoming a shame soldier myself. And two, I had unknowingly been exploring the antidote to shame culture for the last three years.

◎

"The cure for shame is empathy," Jon Ronson writes in the afterword of *So You've Been Publicly Shamed*. I fully agree. The more we see each other as human, the harder it becomes to shame each other. Unfortunately, I don't believe that empathy—*real* empathy—can be taught, or cultivated through mandate. Nor do I think it can be fostered through shirts that feature the word *empathy* in fun colors or a bumper sticker that reads "empathy for the win," or even a chapter in a book titled "Empathy Is not Endorsement." Fortunately, however, I do believe that there are places where empathy thrives. And one such place is conversation.

Just as I have found that conversation is the antidote to both the game of the internet and the sport of debate, I also see it as the most potent antidote to shame. By removing a points system and allowing room for nuance and complexity, conversation is able to humanize all those involved, a feature that shame culture lacks. And when we see each other as human beings—not as opponents, targets, or punching bags—we are more inclined to embrace redemption over excommunication. If debate sees wrongdoing as a cause for a battle, and shame sees it as grounds for expulsion and humiliation, then conversation sees transgression as a call for further understanding.

The idea of counteracting shame with dialogue isn't new at all. The culture of shame is sometimes referred to as "call-out culture" and the activist and professor Loretta J. Ross has long advocated for the notion of calling people *in* instead.

"Call-outs make people fearful of being targeted. People avoid meaningful conversations when hypervigilant perfectionists point out apparent mistakes, feeding the cannibalistic maw of the cancel culture," Ross wrote in a 2019 *New York Times* op-ed. "We can change this culture. Calling-in is simply a call-out done with love. Some corrections can be made privately. Others will necessarily be public, but done with respect."

By making direct contact with my paper-discarding neighbors, I had opted for a restorative approach to their "wrongdoing" rather than a punitive one. By reaching out to them privately, rather than shaming them through a public sign on our communal lamppost, I had chosen communication over humiliation. How had this decision taken me so long? Why was this not my first instinct? Hadn't I spent the last three years of my life dedicating myself to doing exactly this?

Conversations with People Who Hate Me was never intentionally meant to be about shame. At least not at the beginning. The word "shame" was nowhere to be found in any of my early writings about the podcast, why I started it, and my purpose in continuing it. The project began as a personal coping mechanism, a way for me to process my ever-growing HATE FOLDER and humanize my detractors by speaking with them one-on-one. Only organically did it become a template for dialogue across disagreement. Now, though, I can see how the phone calls I've had and hosted for the podcast also offer a clear alternative to shame culture. By reaching out to my detractors rather than humiliating them, I was able to more productively reach them. By refusing to shame them—by honoring their various requests for anonymity and treating them as human beings rather than "trolls"—I unknowingly participated in an anti-shame model. If shame culture demands accountability through humiliation, then my phone calls argue that conversation is a form of accountability with love.

To many, accountability looks like an apology. But in my experience, conversation is apology in action. Even if it's messy, even if it's awkward at times, even if the words "I'm sorry" are never uttered once. Of course, I'm referring to *true* conversation; not debate, not interrogation, not even a phone call trapped in the Everything Storm, but a dance—a peaceful exchange between humans who are genuinely trying to understand each other and be understood. For me, not even the most poetic mea culpa could compare to Josh allowing me to get to know him after he called me "a moron" or Frank explaining why he called me a "piece of shit." Not even the most genuine "I'm sorry" could rival Adam calmly walking me through the foundations of his faith or E opening up to me about his childhood. Knowing is the antidote to fear and fear thrives on distance. Conversation minimizes that distance. And because my guests agreed to speak with me—allowing me to see them fully and therefore know them—I no longer feared them. And because I no longer feared them, I could forgive them.

Forgiveness is tricky, though, as it can only be granted by the person who was wronged. In other words, we can only accept apologies—in whatever form they may present themselves—if they're directed to us. I cannot determine if the phone call with Jonathan was sufficient for Emma to forgive him for calling her a liar, nor do I have the authority to request that Jonathan forgive K for publicly wishing he was eaten alive by wild dogs simply because she agreed to speak with him. For that matter, I can't tell K that she ought to give Jonathan a fair shot just because he was down to talk with her. That is up to each of them to decide for themselves. Still, the dance floor of conversation creates more supportive ground for forgiveness to happen and this support acts as a deterrent to shame.

So, if conversation is so incredible, and shame is so bad, then why don't we always choose connection over humiliation? Because of one big problem: Shame is a natural impulse. In fact, it's practically our default response to wrongdoing. I myself am a prime example. Before I began talking to my detractors, my first instinct was to share screenshots from the HATE FOLDER and poke fun at their typos and faulty logic. Only when that proved to be unrewarding did I decide to connect with them rather than humiliate them in retaliation. But I apparently didn't internalize this lesson because even after devoting myself for years to a social experiment that practiced a form of "calling in" and digital restorative justice, my reflexive response in addressing the slightest wrongs of my neighbors was to reach for the very weapons that I had watched shame soldiers use so callously. Shame is sadly our reflex.

So, how do we address this culture of shame? Do we simply shame the shamers? Do we aggressively tweet all-caps proclamations that say "FRIENDLY REMINDER TO STOP SHAMING PEOPLE" and hope it goes viral? Or do we submit to the power of shame armies and begrudgingly join them? Perhaps the solution can come from my recycling saga with my neighbors. Specifically, what *stopped* me from shaming them. I didn't refrain from humiliating them because I'm a saint or a paragon of human acceptance. Instead, I opted to make direct contact rather than calling them out because of my self-interested desire to keep the peace in my neighborhood.

A physical neighborhood is essentially a network of human beings who are all accountable to each other—a group of many types of people who make many types of mistakes, but whose well-being is ultimately tied up together. My day will be worse if the person next door is upset with me, I won't be able to sleep if the tenant upstairs has a midnight exercise routine, and I'll be hesitant to go outside if the business owner downstairs and I have a strained rapport. So how do we solve these fractured relationships? We repair them as best we can, not so that we can be best friends with every person on our block, but so that we can go about our days as peacefully as possible.

Digital communities, on the other hand, offer solutions that are more extreme and final. We can block people, mute them, report them, hurl hate at them, or shame them; we can make ourselves invisible, change our names, or delete our accounts altogether. Equivalent solutions in physical communities aren't as simple. We can't evict someone just because they prohibited us from getting a full eight hours of sleep and few of us have the money or energy to move to a new zip code at the first hint of conflict. What if we apply the same school of thought to the internet? What if we consider the digital sphere to be one large neighborhood and the people we pass as our fellow neighbors?

Admittedly, this is harder to apply to cyberspace. Physical neighborhoods are naturally limited in size and because of that, it's possible to at least peripherally know the finite number of people who live and work in our proximity. Digital neighborhoods, on the other hand, shift constantly and it would be laughably impractical to regard all 4.48 billion social media users as our next-door pals. Still, seeing all the people we pass online as fellow residents might help us reconsider how we manage conflict.

To be clear, this metaphor is not meant to suggest that everyone is a harmless angel, incapable of doing wrong. Some neighbors bring great harm to a community, some terrorize from within, while others hold great power and wield that power unfairly. We shouldn't put ourselves in danger simply for the poetic fantasy of seeing the internet as one big populace, but I believe we should differentiate between who is truly dangerous and who might just benefit from direct contact— whether through an intentional request, a handwritten letter, or a private conversation. As Sarah Schulman writes in the conclusion of her book *Conflict Is Not Abuse*, "our transformation into a conscious, accountable, and healing culture requires an openness about differentiating real danger from projected danger."

I've had to make this differentiation myself. Throughout *Conversations with People Who Hate Me*, I've seen my guests as neighbors— neighbors who threw rocks at my digital window, but neighbors, nonetheless. By calling them in, as Loretta J. Ross would say, I invited them inside the home they once pummeled, so they could see the dents their rocks left up close. This has never been to punish them, but rather to show them that a human being lived in the digital home they pelted, and by inviting them in I was able to see that they were human, too. It's worth noting, however, that I didn't invite *everyone* from the HATE FOLDER into my digital home. Certainly not those who made me feel unsafe. The man who said "sending a hitman after you" didn't get an invitation. Nor did the person who repeatedly harassed me through multiple forms of communication over an extended period of time. Or the man who wrote in a comment "I couldn't stop cringing and fantasizing about shoving my cock in his mouth to shut him the fuck up." They, too, are neighbors. Just not ones I have the energy to speak to. I do hope that someone calls them in with love, but I don't think I should be the one to do it.

Neighborhoods allow us to see each other up close in all of our various forms—both good and bad, and everything in between. Sometimes we catch the tenant next door having a bad day, other times we hear a particularly loud fight through our walls. On some mornings we hear the kid who lives around the corner throw a tantrum while their parents drag them to school. We might even remember the weird thing that the man in the apartment downstairs did five years ago.

Of course, a neighborhood also allows us to see those same people at their best. How they light up at a block party, how they smile as they stroll around a nearby park, how you can sometimes faintly hear them singing along to their favorite song through your shared wall. Physical proximity enables us to witness many facets of the same person and we're more inclined to acknowledge someone's humanity when we understand that they're capable of both good and bad behavior.

By seeing the internet as a shared space full of nuanced, three-dimensional people, we can more readily offer grace to the many strangers we pass: both the shame soldier and the transgressor they target; the person who praised you for your bravery and the people who taught you why that bravery was a luxury; the man who called a sexual assault survivor a liar and the woman who hoped he was eaten alive by wild dogs; the untouchable demigods that seem to be universally beloved by the internet and the person who is routinely targeted by shame armies; the neighbor who doesn't know how to properly discard their paper recycling and the person who initially wanted to punish them for their mistake.

◎

The day after I leave the note for my neighbors, I take a walk and am pleasantly surprised by the lack of clutter at the base of the lamppost. Upon my return, though, I stop in my tracks when I see a note posted on their door. I step closer to read it.

"To our neighbor who helped w/ the recycling," the note began, "THANK YOU! We really appreciate your help and will do better going forward."

If the culture of shame, or call-out culture, marks transgressors as "trash," then conversation sees all people as recycling—worthy of keeping around and capable of transformation. Conversation allows us to keep the best parts of ourselves and shed the rest. All for the greater good.

12

snowflakes

I had hoped to end my book—*this* book—by unveiling some singular, concise way to classify all of my guests. For months I sifted through our messages and pored over transcripts, closely analyzing every word, every "um," every sigh, every laugh, every flash of tension and moment of tenderness in an attempt to find that one thing that connected them all—some profound truth that accurately encompassed every single detractor I spoke to on my show. Maybe, I thought, I might even stumble upon some hidden linguistic tic that was present in all of their speech patterns, and this tic might reveal some undiscovered psychological condition that would be named after me in all future diagnostic manuals. But I have come up empty.

Each guest comes from a different place, is guided by different principles, and values different things. They each have different wants and needs and desires and goals. They have different experiences that have shaped their different lives, and they each have radically different ways of recounting those experiences. There isn't even an appropriate term to describe the dozens of strangers that I've spoken with for this social experiment.

Trolls, as I had already discovered, isn't accurate. None of them are distant, inhuman monsters who live beneath a faraway bridge. Plus, the word has too many meanings. Some employ it to label members of internet harassment mobs, while others use it to identify anyone who disagrees with them in an online setting. Some use it to describe shame soldiers, while others misguidedly use it to characterize individuals who express measured critiques. The term can also refer to benign pranksters. With so many conflicting definitions, the label effectively means nothing at all.

Haters, as I also came to understand, isn't quite right, either. As far as I know none of my guests have ever been in actual hate groups. And what I had perceived as "hate" was often discontent expressed hyperbolically. Plus, the various comments that qualified my guests to be on the show were each prompted by different triggers. For some it was an indescribable pain, for others it was deep-seated fear that manifested as a digital attack. Some wrote their comments because of religious teachings, or media persuasion, while others did so because of their own natural aversion to whatever or whomever they were attempting to discredit. Some saw their target as a symbol of a thing they detested, others saw their target as the specific cause of their strife. A few didn't even think they were writing anything negative at all.

Even *conservatives* would be an inaccurate term as I cannot classify my guests by political alignment. I've spoken to people all over the political spectrum, and even within those groupings of "right" and "left" I've found variety. My conservative guests are all distinct from each other. Some have been kind and gentle as we danced through our conversation, others have been more hostile and combative as we sparred our way through the Debate Arena. Some have espoused ideology that I find to be abhorrent, while others have made statements that I was surprised to agree with. Some have violently declined my invitation onto the podcast, citing a lack of trust, while others jumped at the opportunity, thrilled to speak with someone they diverge from ideologically. The same goes for my liberal and progressive guests whose motivations and beliefs and expressions of those beliefs are all unique.

So, there is neither a term for my guests, nor a shared motive, nor a common political party that can capture them accurately. Yet, no matter how dissimilar they may be from each other, I have still caught glimpses of myself in each of them. Sometimes I see this reflection in fleeting moments like a nervous laugh they blurt out as they ease their way into the conversation. Or the hesitation with which they regard me in the first moments of our phone call, dubious about my intentions. I have seen myself in the strange and roundabout ways they compose a thought. Sometimes I'll hear myself in their resistance to a new idea—confused at first, then defensive, then annoyed, and finally, after some time, open and receptive. I have seen flashes of myself in conservative dads, outspoken progressive activists, apolitical college students, gun enthusiasts, artists, religious devotees, teenagers, middle-aged adults, public figures, private citizens, and even a self-identified "gutter faggot." And if we truly had nothing in common, I could, at the very least, cite the fact that we agreed to be on the phone together at the exact same time.

In the end my only true finding is this: There is no secret trait that my guests share and there is no one thing that causes people to write mean comments online. And while there have been valuable studies that allow us to see patterns among groups of people who share common beliefs, to meet the individual members of these groups is to immediately see them as distinct human beings. No two guests are alike. And when I put it that way, I realize that perhaps there is one term that accurately describes them after all.

◎

Snowflake, according to Wikipedia, is a derogatory term for people who have "an inflated sense of uniqueness, an unwarranted sense of entitlement, or are overly emotional, easily offended, and unable to deal with opposing opinions." In the politically fractured climate of 2016, I saw the term used mostly by conservatives against people like me, which is to say politically correct internet users who vocally advocated for social justice. It was a way to mock those of us who talked about things like feelings and respect and safe spaces and pronouns and trigger warnings. But then I started to see the word reclaimed by those of us who were initially targeted. With this tide shift, friends and allies began to use "snowflake" to mock the tender sensitivity of conservatives who demanded certain holiday greetings, second amendment enthusiasts who couldn't live without their guns, and others who expressed confusion at the concept of gender as a spectrum. Eventually the term was used by so many people *against* so many people that it seemed to denigrate the act of feeling anything at all.

On Memorial Day weekend of 2017 I received an unsolicited message that read "Watched some video of you and some fellow flakes... Come to the conclusion you are a waste of oxygen."

I was in the thick of editing the recordings that would become the first episodes of *Conversations with People Who Hate Me*, so, already in the production headspace, I instinctively carried out my established routine: I took a screenshot of the message, filed it away in the HATE FOLDER, and began my journey through the sender's profile pictures and posts.

Thrilled that another episode had landed in my lap, I wrote back immediately. "Haha, thanks! Why?"

"I am the wolfhound...you are the sheep...we see the world different. You believe in a fantasy world. I have stared down evil," the stranger replied ominously.

I asked if there was a particular piece of mine that crawled under his skin, and he cited my final video for Seriously.TV—the one where

I interviewed a panel of my progressive friends where we "shut down" conservative arguments.

"Try being unbiased," he said. "Have a equal number of guests with diff views. Not all liberal/progressives."

"Been working on having conversations with different views, actually," I said, setting the stage for my invitation.

"Keep me posted when that happens. I'd be interested," he wrote. "Diff views are important."

"I actually agree," I wrote back.

"I take back my original post," he said, after we exchanged a few more messages. "My apologies."

I took this as my cue to swoop in and invite him to be a guest on the show. But as soon as I extended the invitation, he began to backtrack.

"I'm not the most articulate," he said.

"You're doing great!" I responded, genuinely.

"I'd probably come off as a heathen," he demurred.

"No no no," I chimed back, positive that he would sound human and real on the phone.

"It takes me a while to form my arguments," he said.

"No worries. I'd love to have you as a guest," I insisted, also aware that it took *me* a while to form my own arguments, too.

This pattern of me inviting him onto the show, and him politely refusing continued for the remainder of our chat and stretched into the following months. I sent him links to released episodes and press clippings to prove that this social experiment was both loving and legit, but he remained elusive.

In February of the following year, nine months after his first message, I made one final attempt. "I'd still love to have you on the show. Let me know if you're interested."

He wrote back the next day. "I'll keep you posted on when I get a network that would support a phone call. Currently it's very unstable for anything other than simple text." He never wrote back after that. What a shame. "Waste of Oxygen" would have been a perfect episode title.

As my disappointment faded, I came to appreciate the irony that this man had dropped into my direct messages, called me a snowflake—or "flake"—because I only spoke to like-minded people, and then ghosted when I invited him to have the exact type of conversation he had accused me of avoiding. *Who*, I thought to myself, *was the snowflake now?* I loved this little anecdote, so when I pitched this book in the fall of 2018 I planned to title it *Snowflake* as a sly reclamation of a word that had been used to hurt me.

But the deeper I got into the writing process, the more I realized how strange a put-down it was: Ultimately the term mocked people for having feelings and a sense of individuality, which, if I understand our species correctly, is the definition of being human. We are all guided by our feelings. Even disagreeing with that sentiment is, itself, a feeling. And seeing ourselves as unique is just proof of functioning neurological faculties.

What's more, throughout my phone calls, I have heard every single one of my guests wrestle with their emotions as they tried to explain what motivated them to write the message or comment they did. And when it came to individuality, they all wanted to define themselves on their own terms and would gently, and sometimes not so gently, correct me if I mistakenly assumed something about them that was untrue.

So, if the only quality that unites my guests is that they are all unique, individual, one-of-a-kind humans who want to be seen as the unique, individual, one-of-a-kind humans they are, then I guess they are all snowflakes. And because they are not human anomalies, that means we—*all* of us—are snowflakes, too. When I realized this, I understood that what at first was a clever title was actually the most potent metaphor for the end of this book.

◎

Consider, for a moment, a literal snowflake. From far away they are tiny specks, one of many, but when we behold them up close we can see that they are beautiful and unique. Stunning reminders of nature's majesty. I can think of nothing that more perfectly encapsulates my experience of having conversations with people who hate me.

Just as snowflakes can be overwhelming and terrifying when they are far away, my guests were overwhelming and terrifying once, too. When I first began to receive hate messages it felt like a relentless army was constantly storming my inbox and comment sections. If I clicked on the profile of a detractor and found little information, I would fear the most dangerous intentions. Waking up to a notification that a faceless stranger three states away wanted to see me dead made me wonder if they were already plotting my demise.

And just as snowflakes are breathtakingly beautiful up close, my guests are breathtakingly beautiful up close, too. From the moment they first say "Hello" I am able to appreciate them as individuals and it is at this close range—voice to voice—that it becomes clear that they aren't my enemies at all, no matter how vehemently we may disagree. Hearing Josh's laugh, or Frank's accent, or learning the tiny detail that E was applying for jobs around the time of our call, allowed me to see them as human, and this opened the door for empathy. And as I walked through that door, my fear dissipated.

But the stunning design of a snowflake does not make up for the harm it can cause. With other snowflakes, they can cause chaos and damage. They make roads slick, they create deadly conditions, and other times just pose a nuisance. If someone crashed their car in a blizzard you wouldn't encourage them to look on the bright side and behold the beauty of the snowflakes as they fall. You'd call an ambulance and a tow truck and stay with them until help arrived. Similarly, when people fall victim to targeted online harassment campaigns— waves of hate or shame armies that have gone too far—their experience of social media becomes a blizzard of abuse and mockery. It's understandably hard to sell them on the idea that they should engage in conversation with their detractors when they are simply trying to survive.

Jon Ronson used this very visual to also explain how individuals perceive—or *don't* perceive—their collective power in public shamings. "The snowflake never needs to feel responsible for the avalanche," he writes. The beautiful complexity of the individual does not absolve wrongdoing, nor does it negate the consequences of group mentality, but it also doesn't justify blaming one snowflake for the entire avalanche.

Having a conversation with an internet stranger is like that moment when a snowflake lands on your hand and you pull it closer to behold it. You are fully aware that it is just one tiny representative of snow, that with its "fellow flakes" it can cause great damage, and, yet, as you look at its nuances, observe its complexities, you might feel like you are seeing a tiny slice of the universe, while also gaining an understanding of a larger truth. You are seeing both the small and the big, the snowflake and the snowstorm, the micro and the macro. You have a sense of power and humility at the same time; power that the very world that created this unique, individual snowflake also created you, and humility from the knowledge that both you and this snowflake are one of so, so, so many others. And all of these thoughts and feelings last only for a moment before the snowflake melts away and recycles itself into the air.

Of course, seeing a snowflake up close, while poetically beautiful, is also impractical and not how we actually experience them. When it snows, we may be able to truly get a good look at one or two, but it's impossible to appreciate the delicate intricacies of *every* little snowflake. In the same way, while it may be sentimentally quaint to remember that every person we pass online is a living, breathing, three-dimensional human with a backstory, it's impossible to actually speak with all of them. Nobody has the time for that, or the energy. And some snowflakes don't want to be known. Still, I have found conversation to be a vital civic practice.

◎

Today as I write this many Big Things are happening. You are reading this in the future so I don't know exactly what is happening in *your* today, many todays from now, but I suspect that it's probably somewhat similar to what's going on in *my* today: Injustice is happening, and people disagree about what caused that injustice and how we can fix it; a celebrity is doing something endearingly relatable or frustratingly unrelatable and we interpret both through our own lens; some people are abusing their power; political disagreements are dictating our future; and multiple humanitarian crises are unfolding simultaneously. All of these Big Things, understandably, cause confusion and pain.

Naturally, we want to process that confusion and pain. This is particularly challenging, though, because the place where many of us go to learn about the Big Things, talk about the Big Things, and process all of the confusion and pain that come from the Big Things is the internet—a space that, on the one hand, connects us to more people than ever before, showing us possibilities and worlds we never thought possible, and on the other hand amplifies our disagreements by rewarding us for opposing each other with hyperbolic panache. It can make us see those we moderately disagree with as villains and those we strongly disagree with as inhuman monsters, all while we get sucked into time-consuming rabbit holes and hurricanes of information and misinformation blending together indecipherably.

Conversation, though, is the antidote to the game of the internet; it is the umbrella in the Everything Storm, the direct pathway out of the Debate Arena and the Court of Public Opinion's interrogation room. It is an intimate dance between strangers.

Unfortunately, dialogue, especially dialogue across disagreement, is becoming increasingly difficult on platforms that were meant to connect us. Fortunately, though, there is a simple solution to this dearth of conversations: Have them. Test the boundaries of who you feel comfortable speaking with without compromising your safety or energy. We don't need to reach out to our *most* distant opponents, or our *most* hateful detractors, but simply those whom we feel are worth our time, yet still challenge us to step out of our comfort zone.

Throughout this book I have taken the lessons I learned from having conversations with people who "hate" me—and hosting conversations between people who "hate" each other—to create a sort of road map for how to have difficult conversations of your own. I have charted this road map from my own specific experiences, but this guide can be used by anyone who seeks any kind of conversation at all. As I said when we began this journey: Take what works for you, and leave what doesn't.

Whomever you choose to speak with—whether it's a family member, a partner, a coworker, a neighbor, or even your own internet foe, and no matter what distance you are attempting to traverse—whether it is ideological, political, digital, geographic, or generational, all of these guidelines can still apply.

One conversation will not heal the world. Empathy alone will not cure what ails us. Inspiring words will not protect us from harm. But in an era when we feel increasingly isolated, when we speak to each other on platforms that divide us by rewarding competition over connection, conversation is a tiny, enormous, mundane, epic, boring, thrilling, simple, complex act of rebellion that builds a bridge where there wasn't one before.

ACKNOWLEDGMENTS

To do a project like this, you must have a lot of love in your life, someone once told me.

They're absolutely right.

I tried to quit writing this book many, many times. I mostly continued because of the persistence and support of my amazing agent Lauren Abramo. Thank you, Lauren, for seeing what was possible when I couldn't. And thanks to your team at DGB—Andrew Dugan, Maria Estevez, and Amy Bishop.

To my editor Loan Le, whose saintlike patience allowed this book the breathing room to become what it needed to become. Thank you for your guidance and trust in me. We did it. To everyone at Atria— Sonja Singleton, Libby McGuire, Lindsay Sagnette, Dana Trocker, Karlyn Hixson, and Ariele Fredman. To Carolyn Levin for reviewing this book with such a fine-tooth comb. To Laywan Kwan who designed this beautiful cover, and Greg Kozatek, who helped me envision the book jacket of my dreams.

To my fact checker Lisa Dusenbery, whose brilliant mind and microscopic attention to detail left no fact unturned. This book is better because of her involvement and I am eternally grateful for her devotion to the truth.

ACKNOWLEDGMENTS

My lawyer Seth Horwitz is a true gem of a human who gets genuinely fired up about this project. His appreciation for this show and all it's trying to accomplish makes what could be a dry, transactional relationship into a fruitful friendship.

Thank you to Kaitlyn Flynn, for opening doors for me. To Michael Grinspan, Jennie Church-Cooper, Ayala Cohen, Brittany Perlmuter, Arielle Lever, Michael Charny, and Ira Schreck and everyone else at ICM, Haven, and SRDA who have supported me throughout this process. To Scott Landesman, Jessica Sharqi, and Lindsay Ryan, who keep my life in order.

To Ethan Berlin, Dustin Flannery-McCoy, Dennis DeNobile, Alen Rahimic, Alison Goldberger, Corey Dome, Jenny Morrissey, Mark Maloney, Ali Rivera, Alex Fischer, Dan Ghosh-Roy, Sachi Ezura, Nikolai Basarich and everyone at Seriously.TV who supported me as I sharpened my voice. Working alongside you all was an honor.

This book would not have existed without this podcast and this podcast would not have been the same without the early support of Joseph Fink and Jeffrey Cranor. When they invited me to join their podcast *Welcome to Night Vale* in 2013, they introduced me to a whole new world and opened my mind to a new future. Watching them grow their own work was a gift itself. So, in 2017, when Joseph asked me if I had an idea for a podcast I immediately pitched him the concept of *Conversations with People Who Hate Me* and he asked that I make it with their new podcast network. I'm so glad I accepted this offer. Because of their support, I was able to work with the show's executive producer, Christy Gressman, who was a crucial ally in shaping the show into what it is today. I also share this show's success with Vincent Cacchione who has been my audio mixer for every single episode, and Adam Cecil whose mind and friendship I cherish. To Christine Ragasa and Megan Larson for getting the word out. To

Mark Stoll and Emily Newman, who came in bright eyed and brilliant just when I needed them.

This project was able to reach millions of more listeners because of Corey Hajim and the amazing team of curators, administrators, event workers, and Big Thinkers at TED. It's not every day that you meet someone who changes your life and also becomes one of your best friends. I'm so lucky that Corey is both.

To Caity Gray, Jon Stewart, and Chris McShane who encouraged me to imagine this podcast as something bigger.

To Jason Sudeikis, whose belief in me and this project gave me the confidence I needed at a time I needed it most.

To the great minds who are infusing nuance, empathy, and compassion into the public square: Loretta J. Ross, Jon Ronson, Contrapoints, Sarah Schulman, Monica Lewinsky, and others whose work I can't wait to discover.

To Ngọc Loan Trần who coined the phrase "calling-in." Thank you for giving us all such compelling alternative.

I was very pleased with myself when I had the idea to extend the metaphor of shame culture's "trash" by likening conversation to "recycling."

I'm brilliant! I thought smugly.

I was, however, humbled to learn that I wasn't the first. In an essay titled "#Canceled: Accountability, Disposability, and Why We're All Trash" published in February 2019 Kyra Jones writes "We've all been trash at some point, but some of us just got recycled. If we think twice about throwing away a water bottle, shouldn't we do the same with people? The shift from Cancel Culture to accountability will be a long process, but recycling isn't just good for the environment, it's also good for social justice."

There isn't an agreed-upon way to acknowledge parallel thought, but what a cool opportunity to spotlight another writer: Kyra Jones is a screenwriter, filmmaker, and actor. You can find her on Twitter at @blkassfeminist.

To Anne Lamott, Natalie Goldberg, and Jami Attenberg whose writing *about* writing has served as a network of lanterns, guiding a dark and winding path.

To Scott Adkins for welcoming me into the Brooklyn Writers Space where I wrestled with early drafts of these chapters, and to Manoush Zomorodi for telling me about it.

To my first artistic home, the New York Neo-Futurists, thank you for teaching me the creative language that continues to inform my work. I'm proud to have belonged to such an amazing group.

To teachers, mentors, and professors who have made me feel like my ideas mattered: Jennifer Fell Hayes, Clifford Chase, Rob Neill, Jonathan Cutler, Diane Moroff, Donovan Hohn, and Yuriy Kordonskiy.

To my writer friends Chris Duffy, Jo Firestone, Aparna Nancherla, Jonny Sun, Franchesca Ramsey, Nora McInerny, sujatha baliga, Bowen Yang, and Ashley C. Ford, who both inspired me and gently walked me through this process.

As I wrote this book, I put my friends' names on little note cards that I taped to the wall behind my computer. I would frequently look to these pink index cards as fuel to keep going. They know who they are. And I love them all.

To my therapist Paul, who has walked me through every anxiety attack, every panic spiral, and every mundane concern I've ever had for the last ten years.

To every person I've ever spoken with for the show, you have taught me more than you know. To every person who I've invited to be on the show but refused my invitation, even your refusal provided a valuable lesson. To the listeners, who write to me frequently and share how these conversations mirror aspects of their own lives, thank you.

To Josh, my very first call. Thank you for showing me what was possible. Thank you for being one of the most unlikely and valuable friendships of my life.

To my inherited family on both coasts—Annette, Karla, Erik, Vin, Ana, Raiden, Hannah, Roman, Micah, Kayla, Amelia, and Emma. No amount of hugs will express how much I love you.

To Jim Clayton, the world's best father-in-law whose unwavering support I can always count on. To the incredible Nancy Clayton, whose beaming face and sturdy hugs I craved throughout this process. I wish I could show you this book.

To my amazing dad who always pushed me to explore new ideas, new horizons, and new people. When I was younger he would always say "Big guy, have I told you today?" to which I would say "no!" and he would say "I love you." Dad, have I told you today? I love you.

To my ferociously smart mom whose ability to speak to people—to listen to their deepest secrets, anxieties, and fears without a hint of shame—is a skill that I hope to continue to hone in myself. Mom, I love you pretzels and pretzels and pretzels.

And finally, to Todd. There are not enough words to thank you for the way you have supported me throughout this process. You are both the voice in my head that encourages me to take big leaps, and the net that I know is there to catch me when I fall. You are the best thing that has ever happened to me. Simply knowing you would be an honor itself, but that I get to love you and be loved by you is my life's greatest gift.

ABOUT THE AUTHOR

DYLAN MARRON is the host and creator of the critically acclaimed podcast *Conversations with People Who Hate Me*, a social experiment that connects adversarial internet strangers through phone calls. He recently joined the writing staff of the Emmy-winning hit television series *Ted Lasso*.

Dylan is also the voice of Carlos on the international podcast sensation *Welcome to Night Vale*, an alum of the New York Neo-Futurists theater company, and the creator of *Every Single Word*, a video series that edits down popular films to feature only the words spoken by people of color. As a writer and correspondent at Seriously.TV, Dylan created, hosted, and produced *Sitting in Bathrooms with Trans People*, *Shutting Down Bullsh*t*, and the *Unboxing* series.

Conversations with People Who Hate Me was selected as a Podcast Pick by *USA Today* and the *Guardian*, named "the timeliest podcast" by *Fast Company*, won a Webby Award, and was the subject of Dylan's 2018 TED Talk, "Empathy Is Not Endorsement." He lives in Brooklyn, New York, with his husband, Todd.